Power to Sell

Master your human superpowers

by Eric Gjerdevig

DORRANCE
PUBLISHING CO
EST. 1920
PITTSBURGH, PENNSYLVANIA 15238

Dorrance Publishing Co
585 Alpha Drive
Suite 103
Pittsburgh, PA 15238
Visit our website at *www.dorrancebookstore.com*

ISBN: 979-8-8860-4160-6
eISBN: 979-8-8860-4816-2

Acknowledgements

To the families that have and continue to shape my life.

Sara, our parents, and our children;
I continue to learn from each of you every day.

My past team members at Summit Group Software who entrusted me to
serve them through my entrepreneurial journey.

My students who inspire and energize me more than they realize.

Thank you all!

Contents

Power
to
Sell

Master your human superpowers

Introduction

I am a salesperson. That has never been my title—product manager, team manager, entrepreneur, business owner, company president, commissioner, consultant, lecturer—but the lack of a title doesn't make the statement less accurate.

I spent years pushing back against that moniker. I didn't want to be categorized in such a degrading way. From my early childhood, influenced by TV and movies, I thought of salespeople from a stereotypical point of view—cheap suits and combovers—a step above carnival barker—represented by a high-pressure encounter between a pushy salesperson and their target. Two college degrees did little to correct those misperceptions—I learned about legitimate business skills such as management, economics, finance, marketing, and accounting—no sales courses to be found. No education is required for such a rudimentary job skill.

Years later, my entrepreneurial journey started with leaving Microsoft and launching a software consulting company with a good friend and Microsoft colleague. I fell into the same trap that many entrepreneurs do—thinking I'm the product person, visionary, creative, or have this unique skillset or knowledge. We tend to overvalue the 'thing' or 'idea' and undervalue common and traditionally thought of business skills like selling! We treat sales as if it's some rudimentary, single-faceted skill, utilized only in the act of selling whatever whatchamacallit or thingamajig that your company produces.

Many people see the function of selling as a recipe or process to be followed, choosing to ignore the complex skills utilized by sales professionals. Sales is a complicated business function leveraging a multifaceted array of human talents used in traditional and nontraditional selling scenarios, from sales to recruiting staff, convincing investors, and motivating fellow team members. Being great at selling is about understanding how people think, their motivations, biases, and how to gain and keep trust. There is nothing single-faceted or simple about it!

Although it took me a long time, I came to cherish my ability to sell and finally realized what the lifeblood of a company really is, the lynchpin that drives the economics of everything—it's sales.

The Pervasiveness of Sales

We often think of selling as the process of peddling or hawking some item or service. Although somewhat accurate, this view fails to recognize the skill used by a parent in 'negotiating' with their child to wear a coat on a cold winter day, convincing a manager of a new concept, motivating a friend to take a trip, or winning over a community member to vote for you in a local small-town election. We are all selling, all the time. In my mind, selling is synonymous with persuasion, and that definition makes it about as abundant as the air we breathe.

Many people fail to see the similarity between sales and other more sought-after business positions or titles. What is the role of a leader or entrepreneur if it is not motivating others by influencing and persuading them toward an idea, strategy, or vision? How is this not sales? An important realization is that being great at sales or leadership depends on many identical underlying skills or talents. At their core, both require the ability to build a relationship, establish trust, and be persuasive; it's a skill used in almost all jobs. It's understanding the human dimension of business, which is every aspect of business.

You might be asking yourself, if selling is somehow synonymous with understanding and persuading other humans, shouldn't we all be great at it? Shouldn't being a human make us excellent at understanding humans? That belief ignores the fact that few of us are exceptional at dissecting and understanding our fears, feelings, emotions, biases, and thoughts, let alone someone else's. It also ignores the ever-increasing role of technology in how humans interact with other humans.

The Role of Technology

There is a fallacy of connectivity in the world today. The existence of digital technology leads us to believe that our world is more 'connected' than ever before, and therefore we believe we understand people better than we do. Are we more connected, or are algorithms, technology, and artificial intelligence simply making it feel that way? Before we answer that, let's review the role technology has played in increasing our productivity in the modern world.

What is defined as the First Industrial Revolution resulted from the invention of the steam engine in the 18th century. Now, you likely don't spend your Labor Day weekends meandering through the Western Minnesota Steam Threshers Convention, but the steam engine doesn't seem like a vast technological achievement to those of us who do. Still, that view is looking at it through a 21st-century lens. The fact is, the steam engine dramatically changed how people worked and increased their productivity, which is the single role and purpose of technology.

During the 19th century, the Second Industrial Revolution saw even greater gains in productivity through the widespread electrification of industry. Starting in the 1960s and 1970s, the Third Industrial Revolution saw the shift from mechanical and analog technology to digital electronics and the beginning of widespread availability of computers, microprocessors, and cellular phones. Each of these periods was impacted significantly by the associated technological advancement, with machines helping humans do more than we could otherwise previously do on our own. These advancements in technology enhanced our human capabilities and made us more efficient.

We are in the dawn of the Fourth Industrial Revolution, a term defined in 2016 by Klaus Schwab, Founder and Executive Chairman of the World Economic Forum. It is uniquely marked by increasingly transparent lines between the human, physical and digital realms. Machines of all kinds communicate with each other, processes are automated based on intelligence devised by algorithms, and humans interact in real-time with mechanical processes through interfaces. We are in the early stages of the Fourth Industrial Revolution, and the exact impact is unknown.

What truly sets this period apart from prior decades is the unique way in which hardware, software, and connectivity are being reconfigured and connected to achieve increasingly ambitious goals. The collection and analysis of vast amounts of data, artificial intelligence, and the seamless interaction between machines are accelerating at an ever-faster pace.

Few of us still wonder if a machine can replace a human; it already has, no human interaction is necessary to buy a new book, music, or anything else online. Now imagine a world where cars drive themselves—oh, wait, they already can. We have productivity assistants and social companions powered by Artificial Intelligence (AI) like Cortana and Alexa. The Internet of things (IoT) is changing how we interact with everything; my pickup truck just emailed me to inform me my tire pressure was low.

We are all guilty of substituting texts, social media posts, and emails for actual human-to-human interaction. Technology may make us feel more connected to one another, but I would argue our dependency on it is stunting our ability to build meaningful connections. Already we are seeing a significantly increasing number of people experiencing social anxiety. What changes will the future bring with the exponential rate of advancement in digital technology such as AI?

There is an even darker side to these technological advancements. Beyond simply threatening human interaction and our competency with human conversation, technology moderates and filters our impressions and influences our acceptance of basic facts. Conspiracy theories, disinformation, and posturing are replacing logic and reason. You could argue that technology has become a propaganda machine. Just look at how technology has fed our biases in 2021 towards Covid-19, vaccines, fair elections, or voter fraud.

As the world becomes more digital than physical, we must strive to understand the impact technology has on our human society and our ability to connect with one another. Is the lens through which we see the world being manipulated by machines? Are our biases being controlled by machines and algorithms? Are we losing some of our most human skills? Is our ability or willingness to trust others decreasing? Is technology helping or hurting?

Augmented reality and the metaverse will bring many benefits to society but they will also amplify these dangers to incomprehensible levels—by integrating simulated sights, sounds, and even feelings into our perception of the real world. Augmented reality will change and distort how we interpret our daily experiences; our physical world and digital world will become one. Will this lead to an even less-trusting society, where we cannot distinguish the difference between what's real and fiction? Is technology negatively impacting our ability to build trust with one another?

Trust

The foundation of any successful relationship is built upon trust; likewise, our ability to persuade or motivate others requires a foundation of precisely that. The trust of others is created by our actions and their belief that we have their best interests at heart instead of our self-centered motivation. Without trust, we are powerless in our attempts to build relationships, be persuasive, or sell.

So, what is happening to trust? To answer that question, we must first understand what builds trust. Trust is not typically built through a single grand gesture or event but instead through many micro-actions; trust is consistency in those micro-actions over time. In the business world these actions are tied to one or more of five key elements: the degree of candidness, dependability, compatibility, expertise, and customer orientation. Customers need to believe you are being honest, that you're dependable, and have similar values. They need to think you're knowledgeable and that you care about the outcome from their perspective.

Every interaction you have with a person impacts their level of trust in that relationship. Micro-actions such as comments or questions can add to or subtract from that trust. Consistency in our words and actions builds trust. It might seem counterintuitive, but even showing vulnerability builds trust. If you have a weakness, it's a strength to share what you can't do with your customer, so they'll believe what you say you can do.

Ernest Hemingway is commonly quoted for saying, "The best way to find out if you can trust somebody is to trust them." Hemingway's suggestion was that trust is reciprocal in nature, and people tend to trust you if you have extended trust with them. Therefore, if the speed at which we gain trust is essential, we must also be willing to extend trust at an even faster rate.

So, if technology negatively impacts trust but plays an increasing role in how we interact, how are businesses supposed to evolve? How can we realize the benefits of technology while limiting these negative and sabotaging aspects? To answer these questions, we must first understand the role that both people and technology play in how companies work.

People, Process, and Tools

Given the complexity of business, having a simple means to understand how they work is essential. A company consists of only three types of people: owners, workers, and customers. Employees and vendors are all workers. Customers might be businesses, but people make their decisions. Everybody gets something, and everybody gives something; customers get value in exchange for money, workers get compensation for their time and skills, and owners get profits for taking a risk and making an investment. Sales drive the entire financial model.

Additionally, every business is made up of numerous business functions. These functions almost entirely rely on people, processes, and tools along with inputs and outputs. People utilize tools and inputs within a business process to deliver outputs. It is that simple, and it's how it always has and always will work. Here is an example.

My great-grandfather was a carpenter in the early 1900s. His ability to build more barns in rural North Dakota was a function of raw materials and time. The more time each task in the process took (such as hand sawing boards or pounding nails), the fewer buildings and less overall income he would make. The tools and processes available at that time largely impacted the amount of labor (time) required; it was a far more labor-intensive process than today. Today, ask a carpenter to build you a house with only handsaws and hammers, and you'd be laughed out of the room.

Tools are about increasing the efficiency of humans in a process or task. Efficiency in a process is achieved by creating more output at a lower cost per unit through lowering the number of inputs, decreasing the necessary time, or eliminating waste involved in a process.

I tend to use the word tool and technology interchangeably. I don't mean to confuse anyone, but a computer is no less a tool than a hammer or a saw; it just does a different job. Both have created the world we live in at the hands of skilled humans.

Accepting this view that people, processes, and tools make up every business function brings up an interesting topic. Human evolution is happening significantly slower than advances in technology; I might be taller and live longer than my great-grandfather but only incrementally at best. Alternatively, tools have improved rapidly, cost less, work longer, don't complain, and are more consistent than humans.

Rapidly advancing technology will motivate business owners to automate processes that don't require human involvement because this investment will pay them a higher overall return. Therefore, as technology improves, it will continue to take over more workloads that humans have traditionally done, it already has, and the pace of change is quickening.

Vernor Vinge wrote in his 1993 essay "The Coming Technological Singularity" that singularity will happen when artificial intelligence surpasses human intelligence. The suggestion is that singularity is a hypothetical point in time at which technology becomes uncontrollable and irreversible, resulting in undreamed-of changes to human civilization. The new super-intelligent technology would continue to upgrade itself and would advance at an incomprehensible rate. Now the concept of singularity can be debated, but it does bring up some interesting questions and concerns; primarily, will technology such as AI ultimately be helpful or destructive to humankind?

If you are mentally picturing yourself fighting a covert war against HAL, Skynet, or the Matrix, let me pull you back into a more hopeful and promising reality. I do not believe that our future includes a battle for supremacy between humans and machines. The Luddite Rebellion of the early 1800s showed us that machines win, not because of their superiority to humans but because owners will always make investments to automate business functions when possible. It pays them a higher return on investment.

The unsuccessful efforts of the Luddites to sabotage or destroy the textile machines didn't stop the textile industry from automation. Since the beginning of the Industrial Revolution, technology has continued to be an ongoing threat to the economic security and viability of the working class; machines are doing what machines do—driving efficiency and automating lower-value tasks and skills. It's easy to see how machines are replacing human jobs, but with new technology we have also created new industries and jobs.

It's important to remember that technology's sole purpose is to serve humans by increasing our efficiency, knowledge, and capabilities. Technology helps us do more, but technology is owned by people, organizations, governments, and businesses; further supporting the idea that its primary function is to serve. Fearing technology and the economic changes it drives is fruitless; a more rational fear would be how less honorable or righteous humans may choose to utilize its power.

With any technological disruption, there will always be winners and losers. As technology plays an ever-increasing role in supporting business processes and improving human efficiency, we must focus on developing the skills and attributes that technology can't replace. Focus on the skills that allow us to build relationships, trust, engage and influence one another. These skills are becoming scarcer as humans leverage technology and replace real human interaction with social media, avatars, and the metaverse. Focus on developing your uniquely human skills, or as I prefer, our superpowers.

Superpowers

Some of you just cringed and are contemplating whether to read any further. Superpowers, you say. Let me ask you this, what do you call the abilities that only humans have? The skills that are duplicated nowhere else in our known universe. The skills that machines are largely incapable of reproducing. To me, these are the closest things we have to superpowers. We shouldn't be cavalier in how we describe or think of them.

In sales, these superpowers allow us to utilize a human-centered approach to achieve differentiation through how we sell, not just by the characteristics, features, and benefits of what we sell. We can all relate to being 'right' and still losing the argument, just like salespeople can offer the best product or price and still fall short of winning the deal. Conversely, understanding how to differentiate yourself as a sales professional through your actions and skills instead of your product or price allows you to win the deals you otherwise might lose. It enables you to stop discounting deals, which is effectively a tax for those who can't differentiate. It's a far more powerful strategy to differentiate based on how you sell, versus what you sell.

What if you could develop and perfect the Loki-like ability to quickly gain trust and persuade people's beliefs, attitudes, intentions, motivations, or behaviors? What if this ability to persuade required the extrasensory powers of perception and attunement, the ability to understand what the other person was thinking and feeling? Would this make you an Asgardian or just a damn good salesperson, leader, or entrepreneur?

Humans possess the unique ability to learn and apply our knowledge and experience combined with critical thinking, holistic reasoning, creativity, and emotional intelligence. We must leverage those skills together with technology like artificial intelligence, not in fear of it.

Future Gazing

Technology has unquestionably transformed the role of sales professionals and business professionals alike. Early technology gave us more efficient communication (phone) and more accessible travel (train, automobile, and airplanes). Digital technology such as computers, mobile devices, and the internet allowed us to capture information in databases and made information universally available to everyone. Today, connectivity, automation, sales engagement, and AI provide richer experiences. None of this eliminates the sales professional's role, but it does dramatically change it.

Tools (i.e., technology) are helping to drive efficiency by automating specific lower-value tasks to free up time for more high-value tasks. That is the exact purpose of technology. Advancing technology such as artificial intelligence might be great at rational thinking and problem-solving; technology already dominates in analyzing big data but struggles as the data gets sparser and requires more qualitative analysis. I firmly believe that humans will always play an important role in understanding other humans' emotional, messy, and irrational decision-making.

Artificial intelligence will change humans' jobs dramatically, but its purpose will be to serve us. By doing tedious jobs for us, AI is helping us to improve or focus on our creative skills, hence making humans even more intelligent than ever before. A notable example is DNA sequencing; AI frees genomic experts from tedious and monotonous tasks and improves precision. The use of AI lowers costs, increases outcomes, augments human capabilities, and benefits society.

Now, if you have taken anything that I've written to suggest that I am opposed to technological advancements, that would be a huge misunderstanding. The successful organizations of the future will implement everything that machines can affordably do better than humans while helping their sellers and leaders master their human superpowers. Yes, this means that the sales job of order taker or talking brochure is already close to dead, but salespeople will continue to play a critical role in connecting with and understanding people. We just must not let technology dehumanize the sales conversation and relationship.

The successful sales professional of the future will leverage technology to enhance their superpowers instead of letting technology erode them. Artificial intelligence will enhance our human intelligence. Sales professionals will become digital warriors instead of road warriors; their superpowers will be enhanced or amplified through the greater efficiency that technology will provide. Technology will provide sellers of the future the power to sell more than they otherwise could.

If you haven't already figured it out, this book isn't your typical and predictable guide to making more prospect calls, improving your negotiation tactics, or refining your closing techniques. Many books focus on the nuts and bolts of selling or the ubiquitous steps in a multi-pronged sales process, but this book focuses on what I believe is a far more critical set of skills. These skills are not about being more aggressive, pushy, or salesy, but they are about how to use your human powers to build trust, better understanding, and serve your prospects.

The rest of this book will focus on the skills that collectively give you the power to sell in addition to lead, motivate, and persuade. These powers are not limited to those outcomes. Some are the foundation of all human knowledge. They have given us the world we live in, including the machines and technology that will eventually automate many of the tasks and jobs we do. They are also the skills that will help you in every human relationship.

Throughout the remainder of this book, we'll focus on what I believe are our most essential superpowers. This is not meant to be an all-inclusive list, but I do believe these are our most important skills we can develop as humans. Products and ideas will come and go, but these powers are timeless. We'll break these powers into three categories.

Our Level 1 powers are very foundational in nature, such as asking questions, listening, and storytelling. I know those sound mundane at best, but most people fail miserably at fully mastering these vital skills. You might think that machines can ask questions and listen better than humans, but that view assumes the point, and associated value, is only to capture the stated answer to those questions, which it's not. The answer to many questions is far more complex than the facts provided. Additionally, it's our ability to ask questions and tell stories that have been responsible for the creation and sharing of knowledge throughout history.

Our Level 2 powers will focus on more challenging or difficult skills to develop but these skills will pay you back huge dividends throughout your life: We'll focus on understanding the importance of framing, serving, focus, and anticipation. As an example, I spent 13 years selling Microsoft Dynamics and my company's ability to reframe how the customer saw their purchase decision was key to our success. We'll dive deeper into that in a later section.

Finally, our Level 3 powers are the hardest to master, and they represent skills or traits that we can continually improve. We'll dive into the importance of empathy, truth, courage, and dreaming. Throughout, we'll talk about how these skills are interconnected and collectively how they assist you in building relationships, trust, and persuading others.

In a universe full of superpowers, we must also realize that things hold us back; forces exist that function as effectively Kryptonite in our journey to master these abilities. These forces counter-react our superpowers and often hold us back from achieving success. We'll discuss these opposing forces and how you can succeed despite them in each section.

Let tools do what tools can do so humans can do what ONLY humans can do. Master your human superpowers.

Level 1 Powers

Power of Questions

"If I had an hour to solve a problem and my life depended on the solution, I would spend the first 55 minutes determining the proper question to ask... for once I know the proper question, I could solve the problem in less than five minutes."

- Albert Einstein

When my son was younger, he asked a lot of questions. I remember one day when he was maybe 4, we had the following dialogue.

"Dad, why does the dog lick its butt?" "Ahh...to keep itself clean." *"Dad, can I lick my butt?"* "NO! Absolutely not." *"Why not?"*

If you have ever had children or spent any measurable amount of time with a four- or five-year-old, you know they ask a LOT of questions!

We all start as super-questioners, but it's 'trained' out of us over time. This is unfortunate given that the collective knowledge of the human species—every fact or theory in existence—is the result of first asking a question. Questions are powerful!

Regrettably, many people in business are afraid to ask too many questions. We don't want to seem incompetent or foolish; we are worried about how others will judge us. We fail to realize that successful leaders are successful questioners; they question conventional thinking, underlying assumptions, fundamental practices, and their own beliefs and biases.

I would argue that asking thoughtful and insightful questions that lead a prospect to think about their situation differently is the most critical skill in selling. If you take nothing else away from this book, here are two pieces of advice. First, act more link a 5-year-old by asking more questions. Second, realize that if you don't understand something, odds are others don't either. The willingness to be the 'idiot' in the room could end up being an act of service for others.

This fear of asking too many questions is not just a business-related issue. Many of us move along on autopilot when we really should be repeatedly asking more questions. We should be questioning more about our career choices, health, beliefs, politics, and how we choose to live. Questioning is a form of reflection; it can open new possibilities in our lives. Asking questions is the first step to engaging others, being empathetic, and solving problems.

Blind Squirrel Finds a Nut

Early in my company's history, I went onsite to do a two-hour software demo for an organization's entire leadership team. It was a big opportunity for us at the time. I was an expert at the product but relatively new to selling. The strategy was to woo them with my expertise, to electrify them with our technical know-how.

The company was about an hour from our office. As I pulled into their parking lot, I realized I hadn't brought my power cord for my laptop. Crap! I had an older computer at the time with a battery that would last about 20 minutes at best. I was in a real dilemma; I assumed the meeting would be a complete waste of time.

I sheepishly walked into their offices, apologizing profusely for my mistake. I suggested we use the time to see a short demo and spend time talking through their needs. The circumstances forced me into an uncomfortable strategy; I needed to fill the time by asking questions, and I needed to listen better than ever before. I felt like the whole meeting would be a catastrophe and a gigantic waste of everyone's time, but it wasn't.

The meeting started, and 20 minutes in, my computer crashed, but I hadn't even logged into the application because I was focused on the customer. We spent two hours talking through their needs and challenges. I talked about our solution but didn't get lost in the weeds by showing them unnecessary bells and whistles. Two hours later, I walked out with their CEO telling me it was the best software demo he had ever seen. To this day, I'm not sure if that was sarcasm or a genuine compliment, but either way, we landed the deal that very afternoon.

Telling is not Selling

That meeting was a lightbulb moment. It was the first time I made a meeting about the client's needs and not about showing the product—it's immensely embarrassing to admit that. The meeting wasn't about wowing them with a freewheeling product demo; it was about winning them over with my understanding and comprehension of their issues and needs. A customer-centric approach was far more effective than blindly showing cool features. I learned that the most compelling selling message you can deliver is that you understand someone.

Gaining credibility with prospects is about showing that you understand their challenges, needs, and desires. To do this, you must thoroughly research and investigate the prospect's pain points, challenges, and needs. This has nothing to do with your product; it's about your prospect. Your product is seldomly mentioned at this stage; the entire discussion should focus on the prospect's problems and needs.

Simply put, buyers are less motivated to engage with people who merely pitch a product, but they will open their doors to someone focused on their problems. Make it completely about the customer. The first step to accomplishing this is by asking questions.

Importance of Questions

In sales, every piece of information and buyer insight gets you one step closer to your goal. You start this relationship with a mindset of discovery, a focus on uncovering as much information as possible. This means not letting assumptions lead you down the wrong path. That might sound easier than it is; our knowledge and biases commonly cause us to ignore information or keep us from asking questions. We jump to foregone conclusions, we assume we know the answer, but in many cases we don't.

Questions are multifaceted in their impact on a conversation. The benefits don't stop with simply getting the information and gaining understanding related to the question. Questions are also a relatively quick way to gain trust and build a lasting relationship. The benefit of a question goes far beyond the answer given.

Asking questions is how humans show they care about what others have to say or contribute. Think of how many questions you ask on a first date; it shows you care and are interested in hearing their thoughts or opinions. It creates a connection, and it builds trust. There would be very few second dates if nobody showed interest by asking questions.

Questions can also deliver a powerful message. A great historical example was Ronald Reagan's rhetorical question during his campaign against Jimmy Carter in 1980: "Are you better off than you were four years ago?" This simple question didn't need an explanation. Everyone was painfully aware of skyrocketing inflation and the fifty-two American hostages held by Iranian radicals. People weren't better off. The country was in turmoil, and a simple question served as a potent reminder of those issues.

I recently talked with a business executive with a venture capital firm on campus to do interviews. I asked him what he was looking for in a candidate. His response was interesting: "I think the best candidate will likely be the person who asks the most questions." He explained that the person asking the most questions likely had the most passion and interest in their company.

How to get started

Most meetings start with small talk. In North Dakota, that usually revolves around the weather—too much rain, not enough rain, too cold, too hot, windy, snowy—this weather-talk may seem insignificant, but it's not. We can't help ourselves, just last week I caught myself saying, "Last week's storm was pretty bad but nothing like the Halloween Blizzard of 1991." In that comment, I can hear echoes of my grandfather talking about the winter of 1962/1963.

The misconception of small talk is caused by not understanding the purpose; small talk is the gateway to a better and more meaningful conversation. It's not about the weather. The content of small talk is not the point—familiarity, trust, and rapport are. It's simply a way to connect with someone. Once we have built this foundation, a real conversation can begin.

Once you have established rapport, the next step is to show interest in the other person, and that interest is demonstrated by asking questions. Now, it's essential to realize that curiosity is valuable, but being bombarded with questions can feel intimidating or daunting. Like in dating, too personal of a question asked too early can create tension and shut the conversation down. After all, no self-respecting guy wants to admit they still live with their parents on the first date!

So, questions are vitally important but asked too aggressively can backfire; how are we supposed to navigate this paradox? The answer is relatively simple, start with more straightforward questions, focus on gathering basic information and facts. If you are selling a Customer Relationship Management (CRM) solution, maybe you start by asking about the number of salespeople, their sales process, or annual sales revenue. From there, you ask about the challenges or problems they are having. Once you have uncovered a problem, you can further dive into the consequences if the problem isn't solved; this helps you understand the solution's potential value from the customer's perspective.

Think of asking questions as peeling back layers of an onion. You must tackle the outside layers before entering the more sensitive or personal inside layers. Each question acts as a micro-action towards building trust.

Another tool in asking questions is mirroring. Mirroring is effectively mimicking the other person. Mirroring can be valuable in regular one-on-one discussions and sales interactions. Mirroring shows that you and the other person are in sync, and it can show interest in what the other party has to say. Mirroring helps minimize misunderstandings, increase rapport, and build trust.

Mirroring can take one of two forms. The first is the mimicking of physical actions. For example, the other person crosses their arms, so you cross yours; they lean back in their chair, so you lean back in your chair. This may seem strange but there are studies to suggest this builds a stronger connection with the other person.

Mirror questions are another form of mirroring. Mirror questions are non-directive, which means they are intended to encourage the other person to add detail to what they have said without influencing them to go in a specific direction in terms of content. Mirror questions often involve restatements of what the other person has just said. For example, if a customer says, "Your product is too expensive." You should respond by saying, "Our product is too expensive?" It's not argumentative; instead, it encourages the customer to give you a more profound answer, such as "It's just not in the budget this year." You could dive deeper by simply asking about the budget in the same way.

With each question and subsequent response, you get closer to understanding the issue or need. When you ask a question like this, you must wait enough time to let the person answer the question; many questions go unanswered due to the impatience of the questioner.

A more straightforward strategy is to return to an earlier comment in this section; act more like a 5-year-old. Questions don't need to be complex or overly challenging. I would argue that the more you frame up or define a question, the more limited information you get. Sometimes you should simply ask "why" or "tell me more about that." Don't fall into the trap of responding to their answer by talking about your product, if nothing else, when they stop talking; just ask the same question again, "Tell me more about that."

Finally, you should ask three qualifying questions in your first meeting with a prospect because the answers are vital to your success in sales. You can ask these questions in different ways, but it's vitally important to understand decision-making, timeline, and budget in any sales opportunity. The goal is to gain a high-level understanding of these three items: Validating the customer's and your expectations are in alignment. These questions are about protecting your number-one resource: your time. There is nothing worse in sales than getting multiple meetings into an opportunity only to find an insurmountable obstacle that should have been discovered in the first meeting.

Shut up and listen

Hopefully, you see that questions are your number-one tool in the sales conversation. Questions help us understand the customer's articulated and unarticulated needs. They allow us to uncover information, unlock insights, understand unique needs, build trust, understand emotions, connect, and gain power and influence. This only happens, though, if we listen.

A vital lesson to learn about asking a question is that you must shut up and listen! Silence is okay; they might be thinking. History has taught me that silence after a question is usually a sign that your question hit the right topic. Give them time. If after 10 seconds there is still no answer, ask the same question again by saying something like, "Let me ask that differently." That reinforces that you expect a response and gives them time to think through what they will say.

One of the most important types of questions is follow-up questions. Follow-up questions demonstrate that we are listening and will enable you to gain additional perspective. More on listening in the next section!

When to ask

Questions happen throughout the sales process, and they are appropriate at any time. Questions are also an excellent tool for surprises. When a customer throws a surprise objection at you, the best response is commonly a question. It might be as simple as "Tell me more about your concerns." This buys you time to be more strategic in your response and better understand the issue. I've seen people make the wrong assumption based on an objection and attempt to solve a problem that didn't exist. This often creates an issue that wasn't previously there. Questions are your number-one go-to tool in sales.

Another factor about questions is that the person who asks the question(s) generally has control of the conversation. You are guiding where the conversation goes through the questions you ask. If you feel like you've lost control of a conversation because the other person is asking the questions, try this tactic, say, "I'll answer that question in just a second, but first, I'd like to ask you a question."

Here is another trick I used a lot towards the end of a sales process. There is always that point after delivering a presentation or proposal where the client needs time to review things. Maybe you've handled some objections, but the meeting is ending with the mutual assumption that you'll follow back up in a few days. Ask one more question before ending the meeting: "I sense there is some hesitation. Is there anything else we need to talk through?"

I've asked that question many times. I didn't always sense hesitation, but I recognize a simple fact, there is always hesitation. Take advantage of the obvious when you can. Whether they share anything with you or not, they'll think you can read minds. It attempts to identify any final objections and make the prospect feel that you understand them.

Kryptonite—Fear, Knowledge, and Optimism

Newton's third law of motion states that every force has an equal and opposite force; similarly, every superpower has its form of Kryptonite. If we are going to master our superpowers, we must be aware of the forces working against us. I've already touched on some of these forces that hold us back from being great questioners. Let's review.

Fear holds us back from asking many questions. We can all relate to being hesitant to ask a question out of fear of looking dumb. Our ego gets in the way. I stand in front of a classroom of students frequently and ask, "Any questions?" I know there are questions, but commonly very few are asked. Fear will prove to get in the way of numerous superpowers. We'll talk about the importance of courage in a later section.

Our knowledge and optimism also get in the way of asking more questions. We assume we know an answer, so we don't ask. We are excited to show our product or share our thoughts, so we don't focus on the customer. We believe we can win them over by showing them something instead of focusing on their needs. Remember that telling is not selling.

Final Thought

Questions should be your go-to when you're uncertain what to say; it gets the other person talking. Students have asked me for guidance related to their nervousness in attending the university career fair held each semester. They don't know what they should say and feel apprehensive about starting a conversation with a stranger.

This apprehension is a bias of sorts. Most of us are uncomfortable walking up to a stranger and striking up a conversation. We are afraid. We can all blame our parents for this fear. We grew up learning not to talk with strangers, and we were told the reason was they were dangerous. That is some serious baggage to overcome. It isn't easy, even when we want to speak with a stranger. Imagine seeing someone you were attracted to at a bar; it's a different kind of fear but most people, even as adults, simply choose not to engage even though there might be desire.

Here is the big difference when it comes to a job fair. The employers have literally paid to be there because they want to talk with students. It's remarkable how the simple reframing of the situation changes a student's comfort level. We'll dive into reframing in a later section.

Now, we are left with how to start a conversation. That's easy; ask a question! Ask them what they love about working at their company. It will flow from there. Questions are the first step to mastering human interaction.

Today should be the day you take yourself off mute and contribute by simply asking more questions.

Power of Listening

"I like to listen. I have learned a great deal from listening carefully. Most people never listen."

- Ernest Hemingway

Being great at sales, or simply communicating in general, is about more than just talking. Listening, just like asking questions, is an essential component to success. To listen well is as powerful a means of influence as to talk well. When we listen to others, we can learn something new and see the world through a new set of eyes. Given the importance of listening, it's unfortunate that society seems only to remember the great orators such as Winston Churchill, not the great listeners.

Let's be honest; listening is hard work. I struggle with listening; I always want to start talking, and I'm betting you can relate. Most of us incorrectly associate speaking with activity and listening with inactivity; silence is seen as a void, and we naturally want to fill that void with our words. I'm continually developing this skill and constantly reminding myself that I have more work to do.

A quick internet search gives us an abundance of articles and research that suggest that people retain something less than 50% of what they hear; this is because we are not very talented at listening. We can all relate to daydreaming during a school lecture or having a conversation with someone while watching a TV show and suddenly realizing you weren't paying any attention to either. Listening requires real focus.

According to Stephen Covey, "Most people do not listen with the intent to understand; they listen with the intent to reply." We often think about our next question or our response to what is said and miss essential points or facts, and we simply have too many competing thoughts bouncing around in our heads to be able to listen. Unfortunately, many people have a bias towards action and fail to categorize listening in that way.

Yes, Listening Is a Verb

I find it strange that we all learned to read, write, and speak, but nobody taught us how to listen. The apparent assumption is that listening happens naturally; no effort is required; we just need to be quiet.

We strive to be purposeful with what we say, but the universe leaves listening to chance. Listening is more than the space between questions or waiting to speak. Listening is the other half of asking a question, and they are equally essential components. Listening is about being present in the conversation; it's about making the other person feel truly understood.

Here is an important fact: Listening is not a passive activity. Listening is no less an action than speaking. What is commonly called active listening is an involved process that requires real skill and effort. It's focused on trying to gain understanding and information. Active listening can only be accomplished with suspended judgment; you are not listening if you're thinking about your rebuttal. Listening is also not passively or halfheartedly accomplished. It's a skill, just like playing a sport, which requires development.

Listening Is Selling

Listening is more powerful than most people think. I remember an instance where my company was trying to recruit an experienced developer, and we learned he was struggling to make the decision. It was between a much larger, more well-known company with better benefits and us.

I asked the prospective hire out for a beer, and I never discussed the offer or made a pitch of any kind. That was a losing proposition—I knew the other company's offer was better. Instead, I asked questions and got to know him. One of the last questions I asked him was why he was looking for a new job. His answer was simply, "I want to work for a company that will listen to what I have to say."

Now, some people might think I jumped at the opportunity to point out the obvious—that the company president was out having a beer one-on-one with him, but I didn't. It wasn't necessary, and it was more powerful to let him come to that conclusion independently. After a great conversation, we went our separate ways, and he accepted our offer later that week. All it took was for someone to give him the time and listen to what he wanted. Everyone wants to be heard.

The fun part of that story is that my first cousin was the CEO of the other business at that time. Given their size, I doubt he even was aware of the situation. There is an important lesson here: Winning against a more prominent competitor starts with listening. The simple act of listening can be a form of differentiation.

Keys to Listening Better

There are some common tricks to make sure you get the most out of what someone says. It starts with focusing entirely on the other person. Stop thinking about how to respond, quite the voices in your head, set aside your desire to speak, and never interrupt. This is all way more challenging than it sounds.

Taking notes is a great starting point, considering how little we otherwise retain. Note-taking gives us the ability to review information after the fact. Additionally, it helps us focus on the facts and forces us to focus on what is being said. Just don't start doodling.

Echoing is another technique that helps signal engagement. Echoing is simply speaking someone else's words in our own way, and echoing can help evoke the feelings the other person felt while saying them. Echoing in some ways is a form of paraphrasing. Paraphrasing essential items back to the person to validate that you understood their message forces you to listen. Not only does it show you were listening, but if you missed something, it gives the customer a chance to clarify. It also allows the speaker to highlight further areas of understanding.

Don't be afraid to ask for clarification or for someone to repeat something if it wasn't clear; people assume you understand the message unless you take the time and responsibility to make it clear you didn't. It's far easier to ask for clarification right away versus assuming you understand and finding out later that you misunderstood an essential item or fact.

Listening is enhanced by keeping regular eye contact with the person speaking. Eye contact doesn't mean you are continually staring directly at them. It means, in general, you are keeping your eyes focused on them between moments of looking down to write notes. You don't want your eyes darting to your phone. That takes away your attention.

Saying small things like "yes," "right," "makes sense," and allowing natural silences to happen without interrupting due to your discomfort goes a long way, and it provides encouragement to keep talking.

Like with questions, mirroring is also a way to show you are listening. Using the person's answer to generate your question demonstrates you heard them, and it further provides the ability for them to expand upon their answer. This builds rapport and trust.

A few final tips would be to maintain good eye contact, smile, nod your head at comments that make sense. Don't be distracted by a message on your computer or phone. If someone is giving you their time and sharing information with you, it's your job to provide them with respect by actively listening.

It's about more than what is said.

Many people do not understand that listening is about more than just the content. By listening, showing understanding, and asking questions, we invest in the relationship and show that we are interested in their views, thoughts, or opinions. This is a vital outcome in building a solid relationship and gaining trust, but listening is about more than just what is said.

Focus on understanding the emotion of what is being presented. Most people answer your question with minimal feeling in the professional world. However, emotion can be essential. Dig into it; ask a question designed to pull out the sentiment. Amplify the emotion. Again, this shows a deeper level of understanding, connection and leads to greater trust. Moments of vulnerability can quickly build a deeper relationship. Listen for what's behind the words.

The easiest way to get into the emotion is a tool called labeling. When someone is talking, listen and watch for feelings. If they are angry, say, "You seem angry." If they are frustrated, say, "You must be frustrated." Make it about their emotions by simply labeling them. Don't make it about yourself, though, by saying, "If I understand what you are saying…." That makes it about you instead of about them. Labeling works great with mirroring to get people to share more information than they otherwise would.

Here is another example of labeling. Let's say you are talking to a potential customer about their problem. They talk through some of the challenges in dry, unemotional terms. Based on what they described, it's likely causing them frustration. Ask a question or make a statement that touches on these emotions, such as "That must be frustrating." This shows you're listening to more than just the words. It shows you care about the situation and suggests you are focused on the right outcome. Connecting with a person by offering an emotional understanding of a situation is a step towards developing your superpowers.

Verbal and nonverbal messages can provide salespeople with important cues regarding the buyers' personality and communication style. Sensing and interpreting these characteristics allow the salesperson to adapt their behaviors to enhance the relationship. For example, if someone is analytical, talk more about the numbers. If they are emotive, then focus on the feelings. In either case, it's what the other person is looking for in the conversation.

Remember, when someone feels like they are truly being listened to and understood, it's natural for them to begin to develop trust for the listener. The more we understand the emotion the stronger and faster this trust is built.

Kryptonite—Apathy and Ego

Successful salespeople and leaders understand that being a great listener is the first step to empathy. Unfortunately, we are plagued by society's general inability to listen. Society seems to award people who speak the loudest, instead of people who listen the best. Pair this outcome with ever-improving technologies constantly working to remove human interaction, and the result is apathy.

If empathy is a key to being successful with human interaction and persuasion, then apathy is absolutely a form of Kryptonite. We must beware of letting laziness or a lack of interest keep us from engaging others. We must strive to understand the facts and the emotions of a situation or problem. We must view our ability to ask questions and listen as foundational skills to accomplish better human connections. Beware of apathy. Apathy is a pernicious internal force that works against our success.

As an elected city official in my hometown, I can attest that it's far easier to get people on board with an idea that can be described in 5 words or less. Complicated arguments will almost always lose against a simple phrase even if the idea makes sense. I've lost numerous arguments because understanding my opinion required people to understand the intricacies of tax increment financing. I shouldn't have even tried; the average person won't listen or strive to understand a complicated argument. Apathy is a powerful force.

Ego is another form of Kryptonite that gets in the way of listening. According to the dictionary, ambition is the "strong drive for success," and ego is "an inflated feeling of pride in your superiority over others." Ambition is among the most powerful forces in human psychology and frequently is the reason things get done. Here is the crux, you need an element of faith in your potential to be driven (or have ambition). The challenge is that some people will misread that as ego. So, how do we tell the difference?

Ambitious individuals are very goal-oriented. Ambitious people are not the type of people to languish and sit still. The ambitious person isn't easily knocked off track. Setbacks happen, but this person continues the fight by focusing on their goals. They are defined by their unwillingness to give in to adversity. Ambitious people are the ones that aren't finished because they achieved their goal. They are likely to set another one. They are driven in part by the journey.

On the flip side, people driven by ego are commonly isolated. Their feeling of superiority makes them judgmental and biased. They struggle to listen, much less absorb feedback, and they get defensive quickly. A tool to help manage your ego, make a list of rules—behaviors to practice and those to avoid. Put them in writing.

We all have ambition, and we all have egos. A great way to manage yours is to find the drive to serve others authentically. Serving means focusing on someone else but simultaneously building a relationship, strengthening bonds, and gaining trust. It's a powerful way to utilize what are sometimes thought of as negative characteristics in a positive way—more on serving in a later section.

Final Thought

I've already written how simply being a human does NOT mean you are great at being human. As technologies remove human interaction from our day-to-day experiences, we must work harder to master the skills of engaging with people. We must strive to be empathetic instead of apathetic, and this starts with asking questions and listening.

There is a great line in *Hit Refresh* by Satya Nadella, the CEO of Microsoft. He wrote: "In every meeting, don't just listen—make it possible for others to speak so that everyone's ideas come through." Sometimes being great at listening is about making others feel comfortable with speaking.

Technology could ask questions and capture responses all day long. Still, it would fall short in showing genuine interest and passion for what others are saying, which builds trust and shows you care about their beliefs, feelings, and opinions. Humans are the key to understanding and connecting with other humans. Listening is putting the other person first, which is a prerequisite to persuasion.

Listen with purpose, focus, and effort.
Listen for facts, perspective, and emotion.

Power of Storytelling

"The most powerful person in the world is the storyteller."

- Steve Jobs

Richard Branson wrote in 2016, that "to succeed as an entrepreneur, you also have to be a storyteller." He went on to say that "Storytelling is as old as the campfire and as young as a Tweet." Stories work because they tug at our emotions, are visual, memorable, build trust, and probably most importantly, we've been learning through stories since before most of us could speak. Stories connect with us in ways that simple facts and data can't.

Winnie the Pooh, the Berenstain Bears, Dr. Seuss—as children, we learned almost entirely through stories, not lectures, statistics, charts, or documentaries. As a parent and grandparent, I have read countless stories to my children and my granddaughter, and they educate, in part by connecting on an emotional level.

Storytelling is the vehicle through which history has been passed from generation to generation. It's the oldest form of education, and it's also the oldest form of understanding each other and sharing emotions. It's a key to relating to the experiences of others. This ability to share knowledge, history, and feeling from person to person gives humans the unique ability to advance knowledge from generation to generation. Stories have been the historical way that this was accomplished. What were cave paintings and Egyptian hieroglyphs if they weren't an early form of stories?

We are the only creatures on Earth that share stories. Storytelling is born from the fact that humans are more visual than verbal. Language allows us to move conversations forward, but stories connect us in the most human of ways. Stories add context, meaning, and emotion better than other information-sharing forms. Stories can highlight unrecognized causal relationships and illustrate unexpected or resourceful ways that people have solved similar problems.

We all learned as young children how to listen to a story. We all learned important lessons about life through our parents reading us stories that most of us can still relate to and know. Stories are a powerful teaching tool, both an effective medium and memorable.

Storytelling in Sales

If you want to persuade your customers and create a memorable experience, you must master the skill and psychology of storytelling. Stories provide us a tool to help engage the other person and share information more richly and powerfully. Stories also offer us a means to deliver information and knowledge in a unique voice and perspective, to connect with the person on an emotional level. People tend to make decisions based on their emotions and then justify those decisions with logic. Storytelling allows us to sell the experience, feeling, and potential in a way that connects emotionally.

This may sound political, which isn't my intent, but have you noticed that facts have become almost meaningless to many people? Don't tell facts to influence people; tell stories. Anyone would struggle to pay attention during a long, dry sales pitch that talks about product features and benefits without attempting to connect on a different level. Stories can deliver those same facts in a way that is more consumable, interesting, and memorable.

The more you improve your storytelling ability, the greater your ability to influence—it is that simple. At a minimum, stories help make data and facts come to life. A London School of Business study highlighted that people have less than a 10-percent retention rate when presented with statistics. When those statistics are built into the context of a story, the retention rate jumps to 65-70 percent!

Help Others Listen

We might not be able to shut off our ears, but that doesn't mean we listen. People only listen when they want to. Remember, listening is hard; it requires attention and genuine effort. However, we all love a good story. Properly constructed stories pull us in and connect with us at a different level than just facts. If you want to be heard, tell a good story.

We connect with people through the stories we tell them and the information we share. These stories are much more effective when they are not just dry pieces of facts but follow a narrative. Stories create context and make the information relatable via emotions.

Stories ignite our imaginations and create empathy with the characters and their struggles. Similarly, stories make sales pitches more engaging—for both you and your prospects. Think about what you would rather listen to, a bunch of bland industry-related mumbo-jumbo or a real-life scenario when the product helped make someone's life easier or better?

Many organizations have put together presentations that show why their products are the best logical solutions, and they highlight the product inside and out. However, many of those same companies have realized that being armed with all the features is not enough to get you to a close, and it likely falls short in holding the buyer's attention.

Alternatively, the brain is stimulated when listening to stories with imagery, meaning, and emotion. When demos and or conversations are comprised of stories, the human brain becomes attentive, and their understanding and retention are increased.

Some of the most effective tools in selling are case studies, testimonials, success stories, and even stories of failure. They give customers the ability to understand a conflict or challenge and how you overcame it. It shows how another person or company benefited and allows the prospect to imagine that outcome.

Marketing departments in big and small companies use storytelling to pull in people; successful sales professionals use those same techniques. It makes the process human and relieves us of dry communication that plagues many salespeople.

When to Use

Storytelling is a must-have sales skill. I told many stories when I was selling and now use many of them when teaching. I use them for various reasons, from driving home a specific point to providing a moment of humor or fun. Each semester, the student evaluations I receive commonly call out the real-life stories as positives from the class.

Stories are like tools in a toolbox, you have many of them, and they are used for very targeted situations. Stories related to a topic or problem also demonstrate that you (or your company) have done this before, and it proves your expertise regarding that specific situation which builds trust.

For example, the goal of sales professionals is to help customers solve a problem or need through change. Stories work in change management because their narrative helps people connect new information to what they already know. They allow us to see something from a different direction or through a different frame.

If we think of our pool of stories as a toolbox, it's vital to have different stories for different situations. Some are humorous or fun, some stories focus on success, and some focus on failure. They vary in length, delivery, and purpose. Over time you add or remove stories from that toolbox, and you practice and refine them to ensure they are complete and that your delivery hits the mark.

Delivery

Engaging others comes from using available information and bringing it to life through stories. Storytelling, when properly practiced, pulls people into a dialogue. It's about engaging and interacting with them, and the audience is an active participant along with the storyteller. Storytelling, just like selling or pitching a product, shouldn't be a song-and-dance routine; storytelling must be collaborative and engaging.

Thanks to the internet, there's no shortage of information at customer and employee fingertips. Similarly, your company has tons of experience. But finding a way to share that information and expertise with prospects that engages them and holds their attention requires a good story.

The effectiveness of a story is highly dependent on its delivery. A strong orator such as Winston Churchill could inspire an entire nation with his words and stories. Even just a phrase was powerful in its delivery:

The British people are like the sea. You can put the bucket in anywhere, and pull it up, and always find its salt.

Winston Churchill's power of inspiration was his ability to channel his determination and strengthen his country's resolve through words and stories.

So, you might be wondering how you become an exceptional storyteller. You don't have to be a creative genius to use storytelling in sales; you need a strategy and a lot of practice.

Start with the basics. What are the components of a good story? It starts with the main character and defines the scene. Those two items give you the foundation for the story. Next, you highlight the problem or conflict. That is the challenge that the character faces. This challenge likely reflects a current situation for your client.

You then cover the a-ha moment where the character gets past that roadblock. This is where the story comes together; it's crucial to summarize the lessons learned. Be clear about the journey you are walking your prospect through.

Determine the lesson you are sharing. What is the key takeaway of your story? Knowing your end game makes it easier to build out the framework for the story you are trying to tell and fill in the gaps in the storyline. You need to know your target for your story to hit the mark. That means being sure that your point and your story are exactly what your prospect needs to hear.

Grab their attention. Stories are meant to be interesting, captivating, and informative. Nothing is more important in a story than imagination, so give vivid descriptions and use emotional hooks and humor to engage people fully. Start with a personal and emotional connection, then bring in the facts and figures.

Is the story one you'd want to hear? Use familiar language that keeps it to the point but fun. Make the lesson clear and concise.

Keep it simple. Simple messages that the reader quickly understands are the goal. Remember that pictures are far more valuable than words, so keep it visual in describing the details. Too complex of a message will get lost.

Practice. Practice makes perfect. Rehearsing your story out loud helps to make sure it feels authentic. Tweak, rejigger, and practice some more.

Many people worry about a story sounding overly scripted; does your favorite actor sound scripted in a movie? Practice, practice, and practice some more. If you sound scripted, you simply haven't practiced enough.

Make it personal. Stories work because of their authenticity. Use your own experiences with past clients to bring your message to life. Be transparent and share the emotion of the situation. Personal stories build a connection with others. Speak the truth from the heart, and you'll build trust.

Have a surprise. Just like a great movie, the best storytellers don't want their audience to be bored. It's not uncommon for a person to assume how a story will end, and this can lead our audience to zone out and disengage. As the storyteller, it's our job to prevent this outcome. We must not only keep the story relevant and interesting but also throw in a twist. This can be a surprise of sorts that regains our audience's attention.

Be fearless. The flaws and failures are what make your stories enjoyable and memorable. They make the story human, something we can all relate to. Stories need to be genuine; they prove authenticity and build trust if shared properly. Don't polish every detail: Just tell your story, flaws, and all.

Kryptonite—Embellishment

My son tells excellent fishing stories; the stories get better, and the fish get bigger every time I hear him tell one. The problem for him is I've been on each of those trips and know the facts, which don't seem to be an essential part of the story to him. Imagination and embellishment can make a remarkable story but in a sales scenario are like Kryptonite to the storyteller. In the moment, it feels like it adds to the pizzazz of the story, but we are all on the lookout for fish stories.

Remember, our most foundational requirement of selling anything or leading anybody is developing trust. That means your stories need to be authentic, honest, and fearless. As I have already stated, don't polish every detail, and don't embellish facts. It might appear to work in the short term, but it's a slippery slope, and sooner or later, that fish tale is going to sound and smell a little fishy!

Final Thoughts

A great way to get prospective customers to see value is by presenting relatable customer stories. By telling stories of customers with similar problems, the prospect can see themselves in the story. By showing the prospect how these other companies benefited from a new solution or change, you're forcing them to picture how they could benefit as well. Through excellent storytelling, you are landing your message more memorably. You are providing context to information.

Not all humans are set up to understand logic, but they are set up to understand stories. Stories go beyond simply helping retain the information; they paint a memorable picture in a prospect's mind. Stories give hope, connect with their emotions, and can even mitigate fear. They drive shared meaning and understanding.

It's important to remember that the strongest emotion wins when a decision is made. In sales, that emotion is typically desire versus fear. The desire is tied to a potentially improved future state based on an unmade purchase, and the fear might be linked to either their current state or the risk of buying something and not realizing the benefits. Either way, the strongest emotion wins.

Stories are a terrific way of showing a prospect what the future can look like and how others have accomplished the same goal. When told properly, stories can build the desire for change and diminish the fear. Remember, buyers decide emotionally and justify logically; therefore, our easiest way to connect with them is through a story.

Storytelling is a powerful way to share ideas, engage others, build trust, and help open better dialogue. They are memorable.

Level 2 Powers

Power of Framing

"We cannot solve our problems with the same thinking we used when we created them."

- Albert Einstein

We each view the world through our own unique lens, and what we see is framed with our perspective, experiences, knowledge, and biases. Think of the thorniest issues in the public domain; most are simply about how we choose to frame the issue. An example would be January 6, 2021, the attack on the U.S. Congress; was this an act of patriotism or insurrection? We can each look at the same situation and the same facts but see different things because we frame the problem differently. How we frame information or situations has huge consequences.

Simply put, frames help us facilitate decisions. They focus our minds on what we believe are essential facts, and we disregard the rest. Framing is effectively a cognitive shortcut that allows us to deal with gigantic amounts of information quickly.

Framing involves selecting and focusing on specific aspects of a situation, problem, or decision while excluding or minimizing others. Framing focuses attention—just as cropping and presenting a picture in a frame change what someone sees. When presenting information, our goal of framing is to influence decisions by the way information is received by the other person.

The corporate history books are littered with companies that failed to see or believe the trends and related consumer changes, missing the opportunity to leverage their strength until it was too late. Businesses must be aware of the human biases that can lead to this inaction or organizational blindness. Why isn't there a Blockbuster Video store in the world today; because they framed their understanding incorrectly and therefore didn't understand the changes in the market and the threats to their business until it was too late.

Multiple Frames

One of our uniquely human skills is analyzing and seeing an issue through alternative frames versus solely our instincts. Framing, along with our capacity for abstract causal reasoning (understanding cause-and-effect relationships), is without a doubt a superpower. Neither machine nor other living animals can emulate framing and causal reasoning in the same way.

Sometimes the frame we use isn't the right one; it fails to capture the details or facts that matter most. In these cases, we need to reframe our view of the problem. Some of our most significant discoveries throughout history have been made through the act of reframing, looking at something differently.

Reframing is viewing a situation from a different perspective, which can be helpful in problem-solving, decision-making, and learning. Reframing is where we can genuinely gain knowledge. It's refusing to look at a problem through a single viewpoint by striving to understand new information and utilize a different perspective.

Here is a historical example. It was Magellan who was quoted as saying, "The church says the earth is flat, but I know that it is round, for I have seen the shadow on the moon, and I have more faith in a shadow than in the church."

Magellan lived when most people viewed this through a frame impacted almost exclusively from the churches point of view. However, a new frame was created by reframing the information and looking at it differently. Throughout history, countless discoveries have proved previously thought of facts wrong.

Collectively, our ability to frame, understand causal reasoning, and communicate (pass on knowledge) has created a world of ever-increasing knowledge and scientific advancement; this has enlightened us with the ability to explain and comprehend.

Framing in Sales

In sales, whoever frames the problem, defines the problem. Our role is to help a customer see a situation differently in many cases, and this is effectively an act of helping the customer reframe the problem.

A sales professional provides value to a prospect by framing or reframing the need or problem. Customers today have significantly more access to information than ever before; however, that doesn't mean they have enough experience and knowledge regarding the problem they are trying to solve. As a sales professional, the expertise you bring in helping the buyer navigate these waters is vital.

In complex selling scenarios, framing is an effective strategy to help serve the customer. It allows an organization to take control of the purchase conversation to lead customers to make better decisions. It enables you to reposition yourself as an advisor, not just a vendor or salesperson.

Many people think of sales as helping a buyer solve a problem. Unfortunately, in many cases the customer has identified the wrong problem and, therefore, they are focused on the wrong solution. They are simply looking at the situation through the wrong frame. The role of a sales professional is more than a problem solver; in fact, it is more of being a problem finder by helping the customer navigate through their issue. Problem finding starts with asking questions and listening carefully. It's worth noting that getting someone to switch frames isn't necessarily easy; at a minimum, it requires trust with the prospect.

Once the sales professional is engaged with the buyer, they can break down misconceptions the prospect has about their problems or how they will solve them. It allows the sales professional to bring a new perspective into the conversation, leading the prospect slowly to shift their mindset away from what they perceived to be the answer to their problems, revealing alternatives that they might not otherwise have imagined.

One likely scenario in any sales process is challenging the customer's assumptions about the right solution to their problem. The sales professional can reframe the conversation around a better solution or direction in challenging the prospect.

This concept of reframing isn't really about your product; in fact, you should still not introduce your product as the solution just yet. Reframing can take many different directions, and this step aims to educate the prospect about what the ideal solution looks like without focusing on your product. It seems counter-intuitive, but if sales professionals do this right, their prospects will sell themselves on your solution before you ever have to.

Cognitive Biases

To be successful at framing/reframing, you need to understand how humans think. We like to believe we are all rational actors, but we get faked out all the time. We assume that other people think the way we think. The biggest challenge to choosing the right frame is that we are cognitively biased to use the frames we have used before. Let's look at some of the cognitive biases that lead us down false paths in our decision-making.

A cognitive bias is a systematic pattern of deviation from norm or rationality in judgment. A cognitive bias is a glitch in our reasoning that leads us to misinterpret information from the world around us and therefore come to an erroneous conclusion. Because data from thousands of sources surround us throughout the day, our brain develops prioritization systems to decide which information is deserving of our attention and which information is important enough to file in memory. It also creates shortcuts that help cut down on processing that information. The problem is that the shortcuts and prioritization systems aren't always perfectly objective because their design is uniquely adapted to our experiences. Let's look at several different cognitive biases.

Anchoring bias tends to rely heavily on the early information you learn when evaluating something. In other words, what you know first in an investigation often has a more significant impact on your judgment than the information you discover later. This cognitive bias doesn't just influence sales negotiations; research suggests that doctors become susceptible to anchoring bias when diagnosing patients.

Anchoring bias would suggest there is an excellent argument to make the first offer or presentation; it allows you to set the negotiation terms. Being the first to present allows you to create the frame through which others will be judged.

Confirmation bias makes people ignore information that conflicts with their thoughts and simultaneously favor information confirming their previously held beliefs. Confirmation bias seems more prevalent than ever since a significant subset of society receives news from social media companies that track "likes" and searches, spoon-feeding you information based on your apparent preferences.

This bias is particularly evident in political views. When it comes to gun control, global warming, or voter fraud, people search for things that reinforce their existing beliefs. In many cases, people on opposing sides of an issue can listen to the same facts and walk away with a different interpretation that they feel confirms their point of view; this indicates that confirmation bias is working to "bias" their opinions. This bias is made worse because social media platforms such as Facebook serve up information targeted to feed into your confirmation bias.

Status quo bias is simply the preference for the status quo over change. This bias is the result of a few underlying factors. First, people are generally risk-averse, and change is seen as risky. Secondly, deviation from the status quo can be viewed as losing something, and humans are often loss averse. Human tendency is to continue doing what we've always done.

In the mid-80s, Coca-Cola launched "New Coke," a slight reformulation of the original Coke product. Coca-Cola had done blind taste tests and confirmed that most consumers preferred New Coke to the classic Coke formula. However, when consumers were given the choice, they chose Coke Classic. New Coke was discontinued in 1992.

Selective perception is a cognitive bias defined by people's tendency to see what they want. A classic example regards eyewitness testimony, which is infamously unreliable because our judgment and decision-making is distorted and that can affect the way people remember and talk about the crimes they witness.

Loss aversion is the tendency to prefer avoiding losses. It's a cognitive bias that describes why, for individuals, the pain of losing is psychologically worse than the pleasure of gaining. The loss of money or any other valuable object can feel worse than gaining that same thing. We experience losses more dramatically than wins; therefore, we should suggest what people have to lose.

Dunning-Kruger Effect is a cognitive bias in which a lack of self-awareness is combined with low cognitive ability; the result is unskilled people believing they are much more competent than they are. Like what psychologists call the Lake Wobegon Effect, this is our illusion of superiority, and it's why most people believe they are better than average at their job.

The **Halo bias** or halo effect is a cognitive bias in which our overall impression of a person impacts how we think and feel about their character. We assume that because people were good at one time (their past actions) or are good in one way ("He is nice"), they will be good in other ways ("He is smart").

The **Framing Effect** is a cognitive bias in which people react to a choice differently depending on how it is presented. Here is a simple example, next time you are at the grocery store look at how ground beef is presented. A common label would be 85% lean ground beef. Would you buy it if it said 15% fat? Same product but how we frame or describe it has a significant impact on how we see it.

The opportunity frame is the framing of opportunity cost. Simply put, opportunity cost is what you give up to get something. This frames the opportunity cost in a way that calls out what you will have to give up to get what you want.

An example here might be a client that has a set budget. The client brings up a 'nice-to-have' feature they want that would push well past their budget. By using an opportunity frame, we can push back diplomatically. We could say something like, "That is an interesting feature. We can do it, but with our budget, we'll have to make cuts elsewhere."

The **sunk costs fallacy** (frame) is the tendency of people to irrationally stick with an activity that is failing to meet their expectations due to the investment of time or money they have already made. This is like the person who makes the incorrect assumption that the value of something is related to the amount of effort or cost it took to create that thing. Small business owners know this well, and they put their blood, sweat, and tears into building a business to find out it's often not worth what they feel it should be.

The sunk cost fallacy explains why people finish meals in restaurants even though they are full, watch a movie they aren't enjoying, and keep items they've never used. My wife refuses to get rid of her popover pan, even though I'm not sure she has ever used it. The lesson here is to optimize your future by looking forwards, not backwards.

I would often run into the sunk cost fallacy in selling scenarios. Customers would be dissatisfied with a current solution that wasn't meeting their need. However, they would commonly say, "We need to stick with it a few more years to get our money's worth."

The **reciprocity frame** means that when someone does something for you, you'll naturally want to do something for them. When you offer something for free, people feel a sense of indebtedness towards you. As a social construct, reciprocity suggests that in response to friendly actions, people are frequently much nicer and more cooperative; conversely, in response to unfriendly actions they are frequently much more unfriendly.

An **attribution bias** refers to the systematic errors made when people evaluate or try to find reasons for others' behaviors. For example, we mainly attribute outcomes (good or bad) to the leader. Framing of leadership ignores many organizational factors, and we overstate the influence of the individual leader and ignore the contribution of the team of followers.

There is no shortage of human biases; we've only covered a handful of the cognitive biases and frames that exist. The general concept is that understanding the psychology of the human mind will help you know how to persuade better.

Example of Framing in Sales

Let me walk you through a scenario that was our primary sales strategy when selling Microsoft Dynamics CRM in my previous company. In our first meeting with a prospect, we would highlight the risks of implementing a CRM system through various stories. We'd point out the common reasons CRM systems fail and provide curated content to back up these generalizations. This strategy might seem counter-intuitive, but it was a tactical gambit and was essential to reframing the conversation. It was meant to reframe the discussion from picking a piece of software and instead focus on the desired outcomes and the process that would deliver upon them.

I would compare implementing a CRM solution with accounting software. I'd talk about how accounting software has rules that mandate how it must work (debits equal credits). Knowing these rules allows a vendor to make a lot of accurate assumptions. It's the opposite with sales and marketing tools; doing it differently or being creative is a competitive advantage. Being creative with accounting lands you in jail. Therefore, making assumptions about how any business wants or needs to use a CRM system is a recipe for disaster. Everyone would completely agree because they were already nervous about buying the 'wrong' system.

We would then highlight the need to fully scope out their exact needs before even thinking about the software because the value of a CRM system is when it fits your precise and unique needs, like a glove. So, instead of trying to sell them a six-figure software deal (which would have taken months), we'd immediately try to close them on a five-thousand-dollar scoping engagement in the very first meeting. It was easy to show how this was an intelligent decision and lowered their risk to an otherwise risky project. It also allowed us to sell something on day one versus competing in a long sales process.

So, think through the psychology of this. The buyer is looking at spending six figures on a software project. They are nervous, and they've heard stories before ours about failed software implementations. We walk in the door and instead of telling them they have nothing to worry about we suggest they should be concerned. This is contrary to what they expect and allowed us to differentiate ourselves from our competitors.

We then offered a low-cost form of assistance that helped make sure the software project hits the mark. It's an easier decision, and it's viewed as due diligence. From our perspective, it also allowed us to reframe what we were selling. Our competition tried to sell a CRM solution (which involved a long sales process); we took a different approach. We often got an agreement to those engagements in the first meeting.

When we landed a scoping engagement, we'd send our best people onsite to engage the prospect. We'd learn and document all their needs. We'd deeply engage with them and build a solid relationship. We were seen as part of their team. We'd present them with a solution design. Technically, at this point, our competition was still at the table competing with us. However, they didn't stand a chance because it wasn't about the software at that point. It was about which firm understood their needs best, which was unmistakably us. They paid us too.

We usually cut our losses if a company wouldn't move forward with a scoping engagement. If they weren't going to spend five thousand dollars to take the right approach, why would we ever assume they'd spend six figures? It was a quick way to determine their ability and willingness to decide and commit.

Now, there is a chance we walked away from some deals we could have won, but we've already talked about being fooled by blind optimism; it's an expensive error that sabotages our ultimate success. Secondly, even if we'd won a deal, these customers had already proven they weren't interested in taking our advice or process. Their actions meant they didn't value our experiences and were riskier clients who created a lot of additional project risk. These were the projects that created frustration with our team. Why would we want this outcome? Sometimes losing is winning; it just doesn't feel like it at the time.

This whole strategy was not about bamboozling the customer but making the buying decision more manageable, smaller, and quicker. It allowed us to challenge our customers regarding their understanding of the purchasing process; we reframed the issue and broke up the buying decision into more manageable parts. This tactic resulted in decreased risk, and we brought value by leading the customer down a better (and different) path. We effectively outfoxed and shut out our competition in some cases months before they realized it. Our strategy was built around understanding our biases and the value of framing.

It's worth asking, what are we selling? What is the customer buying? Through framing, we might realize that correctly implementing a CRM solution might be more critical than which CRM system the customer purchased. The challenge is that customers always start by looking for a product; challenging the customer's preconceived notions and reframing is vital.

Framing Experiment

As an experiment in framing, let's evaluate your relationship with your employer. Most people would say the following: "I work for company XYZ." That is how we frame our relationship with our employer, and it implies that the company you work for oversees your job. In my case, I work for North Dakota State University. This implies that they call the shots; they are in charge. Do you see how looking at this relationship through that frame puts the power in their hands? Is that the right frame?

What if you reframed that statement? North Dakota State University works for me. From this view, I can ask whether I can fulfill my career goals and impact the world in the way I want? It puts me in control. In my case, I can then ask the question, is North Dakota State University the platform for achieving my goals and aspirations? That's a very different relationship, and it's a stronger connection. In today's labor market, I would encourage everyone to have a company that works for them. It's simply a question of how you frame the relationship.

Kryptonite—Our Own Biases

It's worth asking, "Is it possible to be completely objective?" We tend to believe that seeing and viewing things reflects an objective reality, but does it?

In striving to understand how cognitive biases impact other people's decision-making, we arguably should conclude that we all fall victim to these same flaws in our thinking. If we somehow could discard these biases, our decision-making would become laborious and time-consuming. So, what are we to do?

Perspective is key to minimizing these fatal flaws. We should pay attention to our environment. Consider the impacts on others. Look for additional information or data that might be available. Seek the perspective of others. Ask yourself, how is the current situation or question like past situations? By seeking out perspective, you eliminate the need for mental shortcuts by thoroughly analyzing the decision at hand. Don't use mental shortcuts if time allows for a more mindful response.

Final Thoughts

Like everyone, I fall victim to my own biases, yield to my emotions, and reason poorly at times. Remember, reframing isn't a skill used only to help others; it's also about how we see ourselves and our problems. Reframing isn't about pretending a situation is great when it isn't. It's about discovering what could be positive, what you could gain by consequence, or how you can use the situation to your benefit. When you can reframe an experience, you can often change what happens as a result.

Reframing is an excellent tool in our personal lives. Instead of falling victim to negative self-talk and pessimism focused on our weaknesses, we should focus on our strengths. Focus on your accomplishments instead of your perceived failures. Focus on what brings us together instead of what divides us. Instead of being mad that you paid more in taxes last year, focus on the fact that you made more money. Negativity can be a destructive force in our lives, or you can choose to look at it through a different frame.

The frame we look through has a significant impact on what we see, how we define a problem, ourselves, and our confidence in finding a solution.

Get good at helping others (and yourself) see challenges in a different light; if you don't like a frame, change it.

Power of Serving

"Actions speak louder than words."

- Moms everywhere

The negative, historical stereotypes associated with selling were born from the view that salespeople were there to win at all costs by taking advantage of customers. The power of serving goes beyond doing what you were hired to do; it's about putting the customer first. The best sales professionals don't sell, they help their customers buy.

In relationship-based selling, the relationship is everything. That means we are not just after a quick transaction. Instead, our focus is on building a long-term relationship and the customer's success (over ours). It's about giving more than we take from a relationship which means that serving our customers before and after the sale is essential to our long-term success.

In relationship-based selling, a sale isn't something you pursue; it's what happens while you're occupied with serving the customer. By thinking of sales as an outcome of serving your customers and prospects, you focus on delivering value through your sales efforts instead of solely as an outcome of your sales efforts. This value is shown in countless ways and helps build trust and further the customer relationship.

Switching Chairs

Serving is a concept based on essentially moving your "chair" to the customer's side of the table. It's providing value to them by helping them navigate information, understand possibilities, helping them make sense of a potential mess, and collaborating with them through rubbing elbows and getting our hands dirty.

It's important to understand that selling is personal. Selling requires building a relationship that touches on emotions and reveals our weaknesses: provider and customer. Customers are also looking to buy more than a simple product; they want to buy an experience.

It's a salesperson's job to help customers buy. Every phase of the process provides an opportunity to create meaningful differentiation. Differentiation is not limited by product characteristics but can be about differentiating the buying process itself by making it more valuable than your competitors.

Here is an important takeaway. Success is not solely driven by what a salesperson says or a product demonstration. What a salesperson asks and how well they understand the buyer can differentiate them from the competition. Taking a service-based approach to selling is an effective differentiation strategy that pays off. Is your sales interaction so valuable that a potential customer would pay for the conversation itself?

Service to Sales

My professional career started in technical support, a job that put me in touch with dozens of customers every day that were typically experiencing some problem. My job wasn't to sell them anything; it was to help them by solving the issue at hand. But this put me on their side of the table and what I discovered was a quick way to build trust with a customer, which I could leverage in a sales effort.

I discovered a lot of sales opportunities through that job. One such instance was in the Fall of 2000. A large global telecommunications company had substantial performance issues with an outdated product they were running and needed it fixed quickly due to a pending acquisition. Instead of simply telling them the answer I knew they needed a higher level of support.

It didn't take more than a few minutes of talking and they asked if I could come onsite. I flew out later that same day to California. We drew out a quick project plan on how to migrate their data into a faster environment. Within 24 hours, I had facilitated a six-figure deal for one of our partners, all through an act of service. That is the power of serving. People like to be served, not sold.

Content Curation

I'm old enough to have grown up using the encyclopedia in my childhood as my primary source of information on just about anything. We had the whole collection prominently displayed in our house. Just about every research assignment I had through high school involved the encyclopedia. There was no such thing as fake news or clickbait, and there was no ability to page through dozens, hundreds, or even thousands of pages of content from a Google search.

In that same era (and before), salespeople tightly controlled access to a lot of privileged product information. They were the gatekeeper to this information, which created an imbalance between salesperson and buyer. This information advantage held by salespeople led to coercive power and resulted in the saying 'buyer beware.'

The times have changed. The internet has empowered buyers by giving them access to an almost endless, gargantuan amount of product information. We are now in a world of information parity. Customers have more access to information than ever before. A quick Google search can uncover endless details on a product and customers' experiences with it. As a result, customers are doing independent research before contacting sellers. Technology has changed the sales professional's role; we are no longer the gatekeepers of information.

There is so much information at a person's fingertips that it has created new challenges. How does a buyer filter through endless details to find the correct or relevant data? Salespeople today no longer control access to that information but need to develop their ability to curate each buyer's correct information. Taking a servant-based approach to helping our customers means helping them focus on the correct information at the right time.

We find ourselves in a time defined with an abundance of information. Prospects (and people in general) have an endless amount of information at their fingertips but often lack the necessary context to fully understand; we are surrounded by so much information while simultaneously lacking deep understanding. Prospects struggle to determine what information is sound, credible, believable, and fact-based. This abundance of information presents a problem for both sellers and buyers. While salespeople fight to differentiate themselves with ideas and insights, customers work to process and make sense of the information available and struggle to make decisions confidently.

Content curation is not just sharing content that you've quickly organized without thought. It's much more than that. Curation happens with a focus on specific topics and specific content goals. Curation requires experience in the field and great familiarity with the products, the issues, customer needs, trends, and the tools that define the industry. To curate requires above-average skills (research, vetting, writing, presentation) and strong knowledge of the matter at hand.

As curators of information, we should think of ourselves as world-class teachers. We win not by understanding our customers' world as well as the customers know it themselves, but by knowing our customers' world better than our customers know it themselves, teaching them what they don't know but should. We accomplish this using targeted, curated, and focused information. The goal is to give the right buyer the right information at the right time.

Curating the correct information pertains to how we present and share data with customers, including the stories we share. There is a lesson here that we can take from Mark Twain, who said, "I didn't have time to write a short letter, so I wrote a long one instead." Sales professionals can deliver significant value by curating the correct information to the customer at the right time.

It's important to understand that the average customer will not work to understand our message; we must strive to simplify it, so they understand with little effort. We must be concise but complete. As modern-day products and services become increasingly complex, so do the sales processes behind them. We can't flood our customers with so much information that they cannot process through it.

More than Content

We serve customers in many ways beyond simply serving up the right content. Another way we serve is by putting the customer's needs ahead of ours. That means, if going in a different direction is the right decision, we don't shy away from that conversation; we encourage it. We encourage it because it does right by the customer, but it also frees us to focus on the clients who are a better fit for our product or service. It's about putting the relationship ahead of the sale, building and maintaining trust.

Handling objections or negotiations is another area where salespeople sometimes have the wrong focus. It's not about one side winning and the other losing. The focus shouldn't be on overcoming or fighting through an objection; it should be centered on addressing a concern and removing obstacles. If we understand our buyer and have asked the right questions, this shouldn't be adversarial at all. Put the relationship first, focus on a win-win outcome, and be transparent about non-negotiables.

We serve our customers through other superpowers such as questions, listening, storytelling, and framing. These are valuable ways of serving prospects by challenging their preconceived notions and helping them see the problem differently. In many cases, it's essential to challenge our prospects and get our customers to think about their own business or issue in a different light.

As many products or solutions become more technically complex, it's important to remember how these powers work together. Our role as a sales professional requires the core skill of listening and understanding what our customer thinks they want and need. It also requires the ability to provide the customer with what they truly need. It's important to note that what the customer wants, and needs are not necessarily the same. Challenging the customer's assumptions and guiding them through the buying process is another form of serving.

Entrepreneurial Mindset

Having an entrepreneurial mindset is about eliminating excuses through accountability. Instead of viewing yourself as a single cog in the sales organization's wheel, you take ownership. Instead of pointing fingers, you take responsibility. You think of yourself as an entrepreneur; you set audacious goals and do whatever it takes to accomplish them.

You effectively become the president of your sales territory. This approach doesn't mean you don't work well with others, but you set ambitious goals and view your territory like it's your own business; you don't let the lack of care or effort from others detract from your success. Entrepreneurial sellers sell themselves as much as they do their products.

Serving others requires an entrepreneurial mindset because most organizations aren't set up to support this effort. It requires viewing your clients the same way an entrepreneur views their first client. Entrepreneurial sellers view themselves as owners of their own 'business' and therefore take more accountability for their outcomes and success, along with the outcomes and success of their customers; it's going above and beyond to serve your customer.

Kryptonite—Selfishness

It's easy to find modern-day examples that make us think humans are inherently selfish. Even evolutionary theories suggest selfishness is related to our survival, where humans had to fight against each other for critical resources to survive. That said, there is a stronger belief that our inherent altruism was a more significant force in our survival. Helping one another, collaborating with others, and sharing essential resources seems to be the better path.

Today, humans still live in conditions of scarcity, with people competing for money and resources. We don't have to look far to understand why humans today behave in selfish ways; we are taught at an early age that we want to be on the winners' side, this drives a need to be very competitive. Additionally, most of us feel judged by others based on our possessions, jobs, and actions, with social media only adding to this belief and feeling.

Now, I'm not suggesting that humans are inherently selfish. Humans move back and forth between altruism and selfishness frequently. In other words, human nature is highly malleable. Our environments largely shape how this is expressed. Place people in a competitive environment, and they'll more likely act selfishly.

So, our environment matters in sales. Put people into a culture where they feel they are constantly competing to keep their job, and their selfish tendencies emerge. I don't mean to suggest we don't control our actions, but our environment can be a form of kryptonite. Selfishness puts your needs ahead of others; serving is putting others' needs ahead of yours and trusting in the outcome.

Final Thoughts

Servant-based selling is predicated on the idea of putting yourself on your customer's team. It's the careful sharing of information and guiding the prospect toward a more transparent, more rationalized view of the purchase decision. In helping the customer meet their need, we succeed in closing another sale and experiencing the joy of serving others.

Remember, it's not about you; it's about the customer. Serving requires setting aside your ambitions and putting the customer's best interest first. Your clients always come first, no matter the situation.

Make your clients feel like you are part of their team by putting their priorities and needs above yours.

Serve people. Give more than you take.

Power of Focus

"People think focus means saying yes to things you've got to focus on. But that's not what it means at all. It means saying no to the hundred other good ideas that there are. You have to pick carefully. I'm actually as proud of the things we haven't done as the things we have done."

- Steve Jobs

Time is the scarcest resource for any company or person. Once it's gone, there is no getting it back. It doesn't matter how rich or poor you might be; there are 24 hours in your day. Whether you're a solopreneur or a C-level executive, your time is limited. How you use that time is critical. Our desired future state drives us. We imagine a better future, and how we spend our time pursuing this goal is a question of focus; what we are focusing on and what we are not.

Success in selling (or any activity) requires focusing the finite resource of time as narrowly as possible on the actions that will lead to our desired outcome. In sales, it's the realization that wasted time detracts from your ability to achieve more sales. The idea of not wasting time sounds obvious to all of us, yet a minority of people are focused on eliminating the unnecessary meetings; they mistakenly see busyness as a sign of success.

Gateway to Success

Focus is the gateway to all thinking: you won't master any of your superpowers without focus. Without focus, we all become distracted, unable to get work done. The lack of focus also makes us less efficient; every time our mind wanders, we are essentially wasting time.

It's easy to find tasks that are enjoyable and interesting to work on; but focus gives us the ability to produce exceptional work. Focus tells us what meetings to turn down and opportunities to pass on. From this perspective, it's not difficult to see why focus is essential for sales success.

As I've already stated, people wear busyness as a badge of honor. They walk around, spuddling about, proudly complaining about their back-to-back meetings and packed calendars. Being busy can make them feel important but it rarely correlates with getting things done. It's an illusion in business that being busy somehow equates to success. It's important to remember that being productive is about getting the right things done; not having a full calendar. Being busy is not the same as being focused.

Don't try to boil the ocean

When I started my company, we had very little focus when it came to prospecting. A customer's size, industry, location, or most any other factor was not a concern; we'd talk to anyone who would listen. Our lack of focus was an inefficient use of our time. We landed some deals, but it's important to remember that even a broken clock is right twice a day.

In marketing and sales, the idea of segmentation is not a new concept. Having a defined target market sounds like common sense. It's easier with some niche products, but it can feel like anybody is a potential customer with more broadly sold items. Regardless of what gadget you are selling, know whom you are selling to. The narrower your definition, the more successful you are likely to be.

Many large businesses will set up their sales organization to serve their various market segments based on geography, industry, or business size. In smaller organizations, the benefit of market segmentation is not less, but the burden of doing it might fall to individual sales representatives. In this case, building out market segmentation and buyer profiles allows you to focus on the prospects with the highest potential to close. Work smarter, not harder.

When you find someone failing at sales, frequently it's because they don't know whom to sell to. The excuse is that nobody is buying, but the reality is that someone is always buying. Focus increases your close rate at a lower overall cost of sale by increasing the odds. You can't be all things to all people. Get narrow, not wide.

The real benefit of getting narrow is that you learn to speak the language. Every industry has terms, acronyms, and jargon unknown outside that industry. If you want to talk with a banking executive but don't understand banking terms like Loan Loss Reserve, your credibility is at stake. Going narrow lets you leverage what you learn from one customer in discussions with other customers. You effectively become an insider to the industry; you are part of the tribe.

Defining a target market is not a Superpower; it's common sense and taught in every foundation of marketing class there is. Having the self-discipline not to get distracted by the bright shiny object (whatever that is) is the superpower. This is harder than it might appear; we are constantly surrounded by bright shiny things distracting us from our goals.

Lead Disqualification

The term 'lead qualification' is like nails on a chalkboard to me, it sets the exact wrong goal; it implies that the goal is to qualify as many leads as possible. That is simply wrong. The goal is to make as many sales as possible, given your limited time and resources. Let's talk through a hypothetical example.

Take two sales resources and give them each 100 unqualified leads. Ask the first rep to qualify as many leads as possible and ask the second rep to disqualify as many leads as possible. This subtle difference might seem irrelevant, but I don't think it is, especially when your compensation is tied to achieving the goal.

In our example, it's reasonable to assume that our salesperson with the goal of qualifying leads will ultimately end up with more leads than the salesperson goaled with disqualifying leads. Let's hypothetically say that our first salesperson ends up with 40 'qualified' leads. The second salesperson ended up with 20 leads they couldn't disqualify. The question is, which list of leads would you rather have?

Would you prefer to spread your limited time across 40 supposedly 'qualified' leads or focus on the smaller list of leads built with a focus on disqualification? The latter list contains the 20 prospects that couldn't be disqualified. A simple change in how we frame a task (and, therefore, what people focus on) can significantly affect the outcome. Focus on the steps that lead to the best possible results.

Want More; Do More

I want to lose 20 pounds. Wanting is easy; doing the work to lose 20 pounds is really hard. This analogy carries through to most things in life, including selling. You need to do more through a focused approach if you want more. A key to success is focusing our conscious mind on the things we want; and then taking the right steps to make it happen while blocking out the noise that gets in the way.

In selling, we need to focus on the top of the funnel even when we are busy working and closing deals. It means that we must serve our customers by delivering tangibles (proposals and demos) and deliver on the intangibles that can differentiate our sales process and relationship. If you want to be the best of the best, you need to work to make it happen, and that work must be targeted at the tasks and efforts that have the highest probability of delivering results.

Wins Can Be Losses

Let's look at an example where failing to have the self-discipline to ask questions, listen, and be focused backfired on me. It was early in our company's history, and we were small; I would have sold ice cubes to Eskimo's if they had been willing to pay our standard consulting rate.

One day, the phone rang, and a representative from a prominent local company asked if we sold Microsoft Dynamics CRM. I, of course, said yes! They then asked for a quote for 25 users and later (that same day) sent over a Purchase Order for the software. It was a great day; we high-fived and had a celebratory late afternoon cocktail. It was like a 'free' deal, closed with minimal time and almost no effort.

The problems started just a few days later when they started asking questions. We quickly realized they had a LOT of wrong expectations and lacked understanding about product functionality and requirements. We hadn't taken the time to ask a single question to help them in this process believing they had done way more homework than they had; they had done none.

We hadn't asked questions, and we knew nothing about their industry needs. We ended up blowing up a relationship in about 72 hours. Slowing down a quick win or saying no to an easy deal is hard! This sale wasn't free; it was free like a puppy. We failed to provide the focus necessary to lead them through the right process.

Kryptonite—Fear of Missing Out and More

We live in a time of distraction. Never-ending notifications, messages, instantaneous communications, and endless information at our fingertips. Fear of missing out makes us try to do everything. Trying to do everything means you won't do anything well.

Another common mistake is letting our optimism control our decisions and blind our objectivity. In sales, few things are worse than wasting your time. It's our most valuable resource, and therefore not wasting time should be our top priority. The problem is that salespeople are primarily optimists who believe they can win any deal, and optimism is like kryptonite in the sales process.

This blind optimism gets in the way of seeing early warning signs. It might be not recognizing the buyer is in cahoots with your competition, believing we can overcome a product limitation, or simply not being aware of our limitations relative to the customer's needs.

Salespeople tend to believe the relationship they have built is strong and ignore the negative signs because they 'feel' or 'believe' they can win.

It's a numbers game; don't let optimism or your gut get in the way of success. Far too much time is wasted in sales, not recognizing or accepting a loss soon enough.

Chasing a deal for weeks or months longer than you should have, is a giant productivity killer. That time could have been spent on other opportunities but is now lost. Focus your time on the deals you can and should win. Everything else is simply a distraction. Be laser-focused on the actions that create the best outcomes.

Final Thoughts

I learned an essential lesson on self-discipline from a businessman named Norm Robinson many years ago. Norm had a saying that stuck with me: "Activity breeds results, inactivity guarantees failure." This simple saying has always impacted my thoughts about self-discipline, whether trying to succeed in sales or simply trying to lose 10 pounds.

One more thought, it takes significant energy to manage a pipeline, prospect, empty your inbox, and close deals. To ensure you have that energy consistently, you also need to make sure you are scheduling downtime. Make sure to realize that focusing on recharging your batteries is a necessary part of the sales process.

Experienced sales professionals are used to negotiating with customers, but they often fail to understand that most negotiations are made with ourselves. Should I hit snooze or wake up and hit the gym? Professionally and personally, remove the unnecessary or unimportant items from your rucksack and focus on what remains. Stay focused.

Activity breeds results, inactivity guarantees failure!

Power of Anticipation

"Remember this: Anticipation is the ultimate power. Losers react; leaders anticipate."

- Tony Robbins

Many people wrongly define anticipation as an emotion. A better definition of anticipation is the skill of expecting or predicting something. This expected or predicted event creates a feeling of excitement, fear, or anxiety. The ability to anticipate and the related emotion is a powerful motivator that pervades all aspects of human decision-making. Thanks to this skill, our brains anticipate events, and we survive as a species. Anticipation is an underrated and over-looked business skill.

Anticipation is not a prediction of the distant future nor a prophecy of some sort. Anticipation is a skill based on our knowledge and experience. Let's take a quick look at competitive sports as an example. Have you ever watched a 4th- or 5th-grade basketball game? Most of the players lack the skill of antici-pation. However, someone on the team usually jumps all the passes and looks like they are a grade ahead. That is anticipation. A baseball player anticipates the baseball's trajectory. The defense in a football game anticipates the next play the offense will run. Anticipation is a learnable skill. It may seem like a magical sixth sense, but it's not. It's using your knowledge, experience, and situational awareness (via your five senses) to make a prediction.

I previously discussed how humans have the capacity for abstract causal reasoning (understanding complex cause-and-effect relationships). This ability allows us to develop and improve our ability to anticipate. Now, animals can learn to anticipate an event based on classical conditioning, such as Pavlov's dog, but humans have the unique ability to understand far more complex and abstract levels of causal reasoning.

Society is rooted in anticipation. We work because we anticipate the rewards of working (a paycheck) and anticipate what we'll do with those rewards (go on vacation). We anticipate the outcome of eating differently or exercising more. We anticipate the outcome of asking someone on a date or sharing confidential information with someone. It's the desired outcome that drives our actions. All relationships require some form of trust, and trust is rooted in anticipation.

Conscious Anticipation

Conscious anticipation as a person's ability to assess and respond to likely future events, trends, and uncertainties, allowing them to assess possible outcomes and maximize their opportunities. It's simply analyzing the possible outcomes of a situation and understanding those implications.

In sales, anticipation is a crucial skill; salespeople must anticipate how others feel, perceive, understand, and react. In our first interaction with a prospect, we anticipate the right questions to ask. In our closing meeting, we are anticipating objections and points of negotiations. We are constantly trying to anticipate the right next step. This requires us to understand our customer's needs, motivations, and emotions. Relationships count on the skill of anticipation.

It is said that anticipation precedes all action. Think of the smallest of actions, like a smile. When you smile at someone you walk by on the street, you anticipate they'll smile back. If you wave at a person, you expect they'll wave back. Anticipation is as common as persuasion. Every act of persuasion is tied to an anticipated goal or outcome.

Often, anticipation is instinctual; it's not necessarily something we consciously think about but instead do. That said, we've identified that it's a skill or learned behavior (like hitting a baseball). So, why don't we be more proactive or strategic with our ability to anticipate?

Customer's Anticipation

There is an equally vital role of anticipation that sales professionals must be aware of; that is the role of helping prospects anticipate. We must help the client understand their future state through our sales process, allowing them to see the benefits of our solution and imagine the positive impacts. It is this vision and its associated emotions that have huge implications on a customer's final decision.

Let's state that in a slightly different way, it is prospects anticipating the benefit of a purchase that leads to all sales. Therefore, we must become experts at helping others anticipate. We do this through various activities; our powers of framing and storytelling are especially effective in helping customers gaze upon their future state.

Be Prepared

The simplest example is a quick story about a salesperson who once worked for me. He was young, and it was one of our very first customer meetings that he participated in. The prospect looked at him and made a price objection. Our salesperson stumbled over his words; it was painful to watch. When we left the room, he apologized to me and said, "I just wasn't ready to handle that." Nothing could have been more anticipated than a price objection; it was a failure of anticipation.

The trick with anticipation is that everyone is different, and sales (or leadership) is about noticing those differences. A good customer relationship starts with understanding what type of relationship the customer wants. Is this a long-term relationship or more transactional in nature? It's like dating; you need to be on the same page. If you're looking for a long-term relationship and your date isn't, somebody isn't going to be happy with the outcome.

Kryptonite—Uncertainty and Anxiety

Anxiety is the fear of what might happen (experiencing future failure). It's the result of anticipating something negative. Uncertainty about a probable future event disrupts our ability to anticipate the outcome accurately.

Philosopher Daniel Dennett describes the human brain as an "anticipation machine, and 'making future' is the most important thing it does." As previously stated, our anticipation skill allows us to predict the future and increase the odds of desired outcomes while avoiding or mitigating the negative ones. This ability is related to our level of certainty regarding future events—the likelihood of how and when something will occur. Uncertainty diminishes how efficiently and effectively we can prepare for the future and thus contributes to anxiety.

We cannot eliminate all uncertainty, but we can always strive to decrease its effect. Ask more questions, actively listen; our superpowers are the key to managing our uncertainty and lowering our anxiety.

Final Thoughts

There are few certainties in life; however, those who can anticipate the future have a better chance of achieving their goals. Refining and improving your skills to anticipate the right next step in a sales opportunity is powerful.

A question many students ask is "When do I close the sale?" The answer is simple: "When you can." It's about anticipation. It's picking up on the cues that the customer is giving you: their comments, actions, and nonverbals. To continue the dating analogy, it's like asking someone to marry you. You don't go into that question half-heartedly without having a high degree of confidence in the answer. There have probably been more than enough hints or signs to anticipate the outcome.

Here is another vital point to remember about anticipation. When you encounter issues, don't guess the resolution. Anticipation is a great skill but don't forget to ask questions. If you have built a trust-based relationship, then you should simply ask them: "What can we do to resolve this issue?" It's a winning strategy to always be direct, transparent, and simply ask.

Master the power of conscious anticipation.

Level 3 Powers

Power of Empathy

"The great gift of human beings is that we have the power of empathy. We can all sense a mysterious connection to each other."

- Meryl Streep

Empathy is the human ability to understand what another person is experiencing and feeling. Empathy is being able to put yourself in someone else's shoes. It's an act of understanding, being aware of, being sensitive to, and vividly experiencing the feelings of another. It's understanding that there is a difference between a human being and being human. Empathy is powerful!

I've written how the world has become less empathetic, in part due to the impacts of technology. We have all struggled through a pandemic, political unrest, and personal challenges—such as family, health, and job security—loom large for many people. Given these circumstances, it's easy to understand the importance of empathy; it should be at the center of everything we do. Yet, it's easy to get trapped inside our own little world and look at things through our lens of the world, ignoring the emotions of others.

Due to the impact of technology, empathy is becoming a more critical skill. That said, it doesn't mean it hasn't always been important. Over a decade ago, the Harvard Business Review wrote that empathy was critical in being successful at selling. We can look even further back into great literature such as *To Kill a Mockingbird* where Atticus said, "You never really understand a person until you consider things from his point of view—until you climb inside of his skin and walk around it."

To break it down a little more, cognitive empathy entails having somewhat accurate knowledge about the contents of another person's mind. This includes how that person feels. Think of cognitive empathy as labeling. If someone is smiling, we often label it as happy. If they're crying, we label it as sad. This labeling of what a person may be experiencing is how we learn cognitive empathy. Cognitive empathy still requires sensitivity and understanding of emotions. Emotional empathy is about not only understanding or labeling someone's feeling or experience, but it's the act of 'climbing inside of their skin' and experiencing things from their vantage point. Emotional empathy is more intense.

Attunement describes how reactive a person is to another's emotional needs and moods. A well-attuned person will respond with appropriate actions, words, and behaviors based on someone's emotional state. They are talented at recognizing moods and emotions in another person and adapting their response accordingly. To persuade others, we must cultivate an empathetic mindset, and we must get outside our heads and focus on what the other person is thinking and feeling.

A Stranger's Shoes

In my previous life selling business software, we commonly tried to solve a prospect's frustration with their current system. Many of our questions were focused on uncovering frustration. Business owners could even become visibly upset about their current situation. Imagine what those people were feeling at that moment. Our goal was to feel the emotion from the customer's perspective.

What emotions are they experiencing? Maybe they're frustrated because their current solution lacks integration between other systems, which causes their teams to lose hours of productivity. Perhaps the current solution is too complicated, so employees are making errors. Saying to them, "I understand the frustration you're feeling," is a powerful selling tool.

Sharing and validating a customer's experience creates an authentic connection built from trust and understanding. Likewise, when you can not only understand their struggles but deliver the right solution at the right time, you eliminate their frustration, you've both succeeded.

Benefits of Empathy

By putting yourself in your customers' shoes, you can better understand their needs and concerns. Our capacity to understand what's going on in someone else is potentially our most important quality as humans.

There is exciting research on the benefits of empathy in many different fields. Doctors were once told to avoid emotion and feeling from their patient relationships in the medical field; the belief was that it would get in the way of good medicine. However, medical schools teach the exact opposite today.

Studies have indicated that when patients perceive that their physician is emotionally attuned to them, they tend to share more information, become more agreeable with treatment, and show a greater willingness to address health problems. Simply put, with more emotional engagement on the part of physicians, more trust is generated, leading to improved patient adherence. In addition, when physicians are more emotionally engaged, they tend to communicate more effectively, which improves patients' coping.

Empathy requires vulnerability and emotional intelligence. While it can be difficult to be empathetic, it's also critical to building long-term relationships. Connecting with people on an emotional level is powerful; it quickly builds trust.

Mastering Empathy

So, how do we master the power of empathy? First, master the power of questions and listening. In previous sections, we've talked about how asking questions and listening are keys to emotional understanding. We can't be thinking three steps ahead but instead must be focused on what the other person is saying. We can all sense this when someone isn't paying attention, so can customers.

Being an active listener means asking the right questions. If a customer tells you something and hints at underlying emotions, don't be afraid to dig into it more. Asking clarifying questions can uncover the whole story and provide valuable details.

However, don't expect someone to be completely open with you unless you've established some form of trust and connection. By framing your questions correctly, in a way that reflects an authentic desire to help, you'll build trust and confidence with the customer to provide additional information. When we ask questions that get to the emotions and take the time to listen, we are a long way down the path of being empathetic.

Many people's default instinct is to help in a form that helps them. Are you genuinely focusing on what your customer is saying, or are you picking and choosing the information you want to hear that matches your motivations? Remove any bias or assumptions that you are making. This means focusing not only on what they're saying but on how they're saying it. Likewise, focus on their body language—you may discover a prospect's actions don't match their words. We are often better served by genuinely being as helpful as possible and not worrying about what we get out of it. Focus on the long game, the relationship, the feeling, and emotion.

Think about a buyer. They have needs, fears, and goals. Commonly, they are looking for more than a sales pitch, and they likely want more than just a business transaction. They want to feel like they are being listened to and supported. They need to feel like you have their best interests in mind. They need to feel that you authentically care about them, which builds longer-term and trust-based relationships. Authentically serving our customers is a step towards empathy.

Take the time to slow down; be present in the moment. When you focus on the current conversation, you are better equipped to identify the issues at hand by being present in the conversation. Likewise, being present gives you the means to successfully navigate challenging situations and conversations in a direction that feels natural to the customer.

So, by being empathetic to customers' perspectives and thinking, a salesperson can build trust and foster a healthy relationship. It was Zig Ziglar who stated, "If people like you, they'll listen to you, but if they trust you, they'll do business with you."

As with many of the powers we have covered, an essential factor with empathy is that it goes both ways. Building a relationship and building trust with a person also requires that we don't shy away from expressing ourselves and sharing our own emotions. We need to be as transparent as we want the other person to be with us.

A significant amount of communication with customers takes place digitally. Remote communication via chat, email, or text can generate misunderstandings. This makes using appropriate language with the right tone of voice necessary. The right words and even emoticons can play an essential role during written communication. The use of empathy in these forms of remote communication is a fundamental tool for establishing a closer relationship with customers.

Finally, empathy can't be faked. Don't pretend. For people to be open with you, you must be open with them. Empathy functions as a two-way street. Be prepared to share more of yourself than you usually would, and subsequently be ready to listen when people share in return.

Expressing Gratitude

Let's touch on how to wrap up a meeting by expressing gratitude. This is easy, express thanks for something you are confident the other person will agree with.

- Thank you for taking so much time to talk today.
- Thanks for your willingness to share so much information.
- Thanks for being willing to talk about your frustrations.

The point is simple: Leave the other person feeling good about the conversation. By ending with gratitude, you make sure to complete the meeting on a positive note, and people remember how you made them feel.

What It's Not

Empathy is not sympathy. People want and need their feelings to be understood; that doesn't mean they want or need sympathy. They are different but are commonly confused.

Here is a common yet unfortunate phrase you hear far too often: "I'm sorry you feel that way." That is NOT empathy! It might sound polite at first glance, but you can't be sorry for the way someone else feels. This statement is a way of dismissing or discounting the other person's feelings.

We seek to teach our children the virtues of being concerned and caring for others' feelings, yet this virtue is sorely lacking in many adults today. Scientific research suggests many of us care more about ourselves and less for others. Scroll through the comments on a news article or social media site, and you realize just how unempathetic many people have become.

Suppose you are across the table from someone upset or experiencing a problem that you caused. Your response should not escalate the situation by dismissing the customer's concerns or feelings. If you did something to frustrate or upset the person, apologize. Say you're sorry but do NOT say, "I'm sorry you feel that way."

Kryptonite—Apathy and Judgment

Empathy might seem like an easy superpower, but that would be erroneous. In my opinion, empathy is on a decline due in large part to hyper-individualism and our online and politicized culture. It seems that regressive politics, disinformation, and antisocial values have somehow become socially acceptable for many people.

We are confronting a generational challenge to power on our empathic brains and build a more empathetic society. Again, simply being human doesn't make us great at our most human skills. We must make a conscious effort to engage others even when an email or text would be easier.

Our brains love to try and fill in blanks. We play games that develop this skill. Our minds are programmed to make assumptions—which are shortcuts—instead of taking the time to understand a situation fully. When talking with a prospect, our brains find a way to fill in the blanks with what we think something should be. In so doing, we disregard the thoughts and emotions of the other person—which is an act of apathy. We've talked about apathy in a prior section, but it's essential that we don't hold onto preconceived notions; instead, ask questions and listen.

Being empathetic and developing meaningful connections with other humans takes real effort. Don't distance yourself from your emotions; this not only makes it impossible to experience your feelings, but it limits your ability to feel the emotions of others. Being honest and open with people you don't know that well can be scary; however, choosing to be vulnerable opens the door to genuine human connection and fulfilling relationships.

Finally, our last barrier to empathy is our stereotypes and prejudices about others. Mastering your empathetic abilities is more than having compassion for people you like or who are like you; it involves showing empathy for people you don't like or who are different from you. Society still struggles here, which is a basis for racism and discrimination.

We often make snap judgments based on appearance or accent; in many cases, these judgments are wrong. What do you know about the life of the heavily tattooed barista at Starbucks or the Somalian worker at the grocery store? A good prescription for gaining more empathy in life is making fewer judgments and having more conversations. Empathy is the key to a better society.

Final Thoughts

Empathy might be the ultimate tool for a salesperson or leader. To be clear, understanding what another person is thinking, feeling, and experiencing is a powerful tool; I would go as far as suggesting that empathy's most tremendous potential is equality for all humankind.

In sales, empathy can mean the difference between an average and an exceptional salesperson. Building connections with a customer on an emotional level establishes trust and belief in your ability.

The art of persuading or selling to someone first requires you to know where they are or what problem they are having. You can't help someone get to a new and better place if you don't know where they're starting from.

If you want to be more empathetic in sales, your superpowers are the key to success. Ask more questions, listen, be aware of your biases, and take a service-based approach to selling. Take time to understand the struggles or challenges people are having.

Develop your superpower of empathy through listening, emotionally engaging, withholding judgment, and serving others by making them realize they are not alone.

Power of Truth

"The truth is incontrovertible. Malice may attack it, ignorance may deride it, but in the end, there it is."

- Winston Churchill

There have been countless books, articles, and blogs written on the skills, character traits, or habits of authenticity, transparency, and integrity. I have spent a long time pondering how these individually function and came to a surprising personal conclusion; they are not superpowers. Now, I have little doubt that people will argue otherwise, and I can appreciate their beliefs about the importance of each. I agree that each individually is extremely important. Although I don't believe they are individually superpowers, I think they collectively make up a superpower; I define the power of truth as the intersection of authenticity, transparency, and integrity.

Few people doubt the importance of authenticity, transparency, and integrity in the professional world and beyond. The question to ask is about the relationship between these traits. Can I be authentic without a certain level of transparency? How can I be transparent without some degree of integrity? With a few simple questions, it becomes clear that these skills or traits are interconnected in their importance. That is why I define truth as being where authenticity, transparency, and integrity overlap.

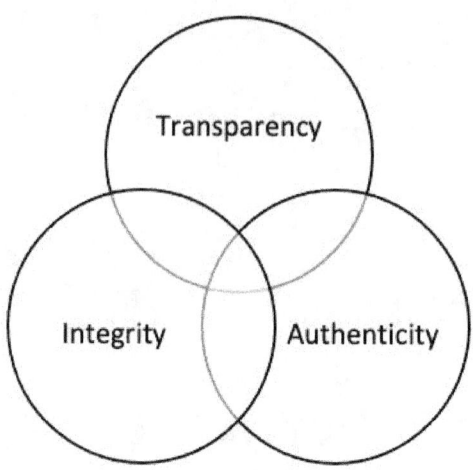

Truth and Trust

I have touched on the importance of trust throughout this book. Trust is developed between two people; it's based on their experience and the belief that the other person can be relied on to do what they say. Truth appeals to reason; it is what we expect to receive. Truth doesn't exist without a degree of authenticity, transparency, and integrity.

Truth reinforces trust because a trustworthy person consistently tells the truth. Trust will be ruined if a person fails to tell the truth. Trust in the messenger reduces our need to question the actual content.

We tend to believe friends and people in our social networks when they share things on social media more than we trust experts. We trust politicians whose views align with ours but lack trust for others. Why have we decided to trust politicians who, in some cases, bend and manipulate the truth? We have fallen victim to our cognitive biases. Misplaced or misguided trust is central to the problem of the ongoing infodemic and essential to its solution.

Breaking It Down

Let's start by distinguishing between the three components that make up truth. All three are essential skills in sales, but sometimes they are commonly and erroneously used. For example, authenticity and transparency are not the same thing. Authenticity is being true to your personality or character. Transparency is being open or honest with someone, not being secretive. Integrity is the quality of being honest and having strong moral principles.

Authenticity helps people connect with customers deeper than would have been possible otherwise; it builds trust. Authenticity is not about marketing yourself to create an image; it's about aligning your actions with your values. Authenticity leads people to mutually favorable outcomes.

Authenticity is related to being courageous; you must be brave to be genuinely authentic at times. Selling isn't about swindling our clients to decide for our benefit; selling is about driving a mutually beneficial outcome where both sides win.

If persuasion is the skill we are after, transparency should be our goal. Transparency is a foundational step in building a mutually beneficial partnership with our customers. It's a vital element in building trust in any relationship and like empathy, being transparent impacts a person's perception of your trustworthiness, which impacts what information they share, how transparent they are in return, and how willing they are to take a leap of faith with you.

Integrity means truth with no hidden motivations or unrevealed consequences. Integrity is not an optional trait! Simply put, integrity is a core value, and it must be at the foundation of everything you do. It's not a switch we turn off when it's convenient.

I think of integrity as knowing who you are and who you're not and being transparent with both. It's recognizing that your responsibility as a sales professional isn't simply selling at all costs but to drive value and a positive outcome for your customers. Sometimes having integrity means pointing a customer in a different direction, the right direction.

You might ask if integrity is a core value, how does the customer see it? My response is simple; they will see integrity in everything you do. They might not know every act of integrity, but overall, it is more visible than you think. The customer sees and feels the truthfulness you exhibit. It's evident in how you process each decision and handle situations when things go wrong. It builds trust.

Integrity starts with an orientation toward the truth. This is where we leverage our abilities to drive actual results by operating from the point of honesty while embracing change and rejecting wrongdoing. It involves being courageous and showing empathy; it's doing the right thing.

Integrity also is inclusive of accountability. It's sales professionals and leaders following through on their commitments and doing the right thing. It's holding themselves accountable to a high standard absent of outside influences.

Here is one final way to consider the differences between authenticity, transparency, and integrity. Authenticity is the what, transparency is the how much, integrity is the why.

Poker versus Chess

I'm not a poker player! I'm too transparent with my feelings and emotions; I'm easy to read. Some people might think this limited my ability to sell or lead; in all honesty, I think this was a significant reason I was successful. In leading our company and selling, I put everything on the table. No secrets.

Poker is a game of secrets and deceit. On the other hand, chess is a game of complete transparency, with all the pieces there for everyone to see. It's an exciting battle of wit and strategy; I think it is the opposite of poker.

When I think of the power of truth, my suggestion is to play chess, not poker.

Persuasion versus Manipulation

There is a vast difference between persuasion and manipulation, and I believe it's based on the power of truth. Aristotle emphasized that persuasion is inherently good because it is a method through which truth becomes known. Persuasion is not about begging or forcing people to a position they don't currently hold; it involves careful preparation, truth, empathy, and serving the needs of the person being persuaded.

On the other hand, manipulation could be considered the perversion of persuasion. It replaces truth with deceit and ignores the best interest of the person being manipulated. Where persuasion is about influence, manipulation is about coercion.

Through notable and positive acts of persuasion, we strive to encourage people to buckle-up, not drink and drive, and give up smoking. Persuasion is the basis of democracy, our laws, our institutions, and it's used in fundraising for charitable organizations and causes. Persuasion is a positive and powerful skill.

Information Symmetry

I've already written about how salespeople used to have access to privileged or controlled information; buyers were dependent on the salesperson to access this controlled information and lead them through the buying process. This dependency impacted everything from pricing to product-specific details. This controlled access to information lowered trust and negatively impacted negotiations.

This information disparity benefited salespeople by increasing their control of a deal. Over the last two decades, the buyer-seller dynamic has changed dramatically; we have achieved information parity or very close to it. We've gone from playing poker to chess, where everything is laid out in front of us. Don't fear this information parity; leverage it.

In this new world of selling, how we deliver value has changed. Today, customers face an immense amount of information at their fingertips. The salesperson is no longer the only option for buyers to learn about solutions and determine whether a product is right for them.

The value salespeople deliver now goes beyond product information and demonstrations. We now must serve our customers the correct information to differentiate us from our competitors. The process of buying has become a significant product differentiator.

Example

Many years ago, a company called me to discuss our professional services. They were an HVAC business, and their software needs were a little out of our wheelhouse. I met with them, had a great conversation, and then recommended introducing them to our local competitor (who had more skill in that area). It was an act of authenticity, transparency, and integrity; I used the power of truth.

I learned many years earlier that overcommitting would stress out our team and likely create a dissatisfied customer; neither outcome was acceptable, either outcome would have cost too much. The best part of that interaction was calling up my competitor to hand them a sales opportunity.

Walking from a deal or admitting when you don't have all the answers can feel wrong. Embrace weaknesses in the same way you celebrate strengths and be authentic in selling. Buyers appreciate authenticity—your self-awareness makes you human and credible. The individual I referred to my competitor later followed up with me and introduced me to another business that we landed. It was because I built a relationship on trust and not bluffs.

Kryptonite—Power and Greed

Truth is easy until it's not; the power of truth is not just about being truthful; it's also about finding the truth. Values and integrity are not simply turned on and off based on convenience. Yet, a large swath of our society seems to have replaced facts and truth with conspiracy theories, hate, and a win-at-all-cost attitude. Facts and truth have become complicated.

People are succumbing to greed and their desire for power. We see the relational fractures that may have always been there below the surface become visible through the sociopathic lack of empathy, extremist propaganda, disinformation, gaslighting, and constant attacks on different groups. Made-up claims of voter fraud have destroyed lifetime friendships and family gatherings by the thousands. When people make up or feed lies to support their desires or beliefs, they have let greed or the need for power take control.

We might be facing a monumental time in our history where facts and truth are hard to find or determine, but the truth is essential. Unfortunately, social media has given a megaphone to the voice of extremism to where those fringe views are no longer hidden in the shadows. This amplification of misinformation has fed our biases, created further division, and eroded our empathy? How have partisan talking points become so perverted?

Getting off my soapbox, let me pull this back to the topic at hand. People are struggling to identify facts and truth, which means we must be laser-focused on doing the things that build trust. That starts with mastering our ability to bring authenticity, transparency, and integrity together in the form of truth. It means we never bend the facts; the truth is far too important.

Final Thoughts

The power of truth leads us to be generous with our time and praise. It's not monopolizing the spotlight but instead acknowledging the contributions of others. It's giving time to others when needed and not worrying about what you get in return. It's serving their needs instead of serving your own.

Where there are humans, there will eventually be conflict. Truth gives us the tools to cut through conflict by listening and understanding a situation from all angles. This shows up with their authentic self, facing difficult people and problems with unfettered, emotional honesty, transparency, integrity, and absolutely zero shenanigans.

When we sell something, we are also selling ourselves. People intuitively trust or distrust an idea or product based on their "gut reaction" to the people representing it. If they sense a lack of integrity, authenticity, coercive intent, or a feeling of duplicity, the deal is dead.

These are not character traits that can be flipped on and off like a light switch. Set the bar high and hold yourself accountable to never deviate. Truth is not negotiable.

Truth is an essential ingredient in effective communication and lasting relationships.

Power of Courage

"Fear is a reaction. Courage is a decision."

- Winston Churchill

Being a sales professional isn't for the faint of heart. Sales jobs involve engaging with people in a complex, emotional, and psychologically fraught interaction. Some people naturally are talented at prospecting, cold calling, negotiating, and influencing people towards a decision. Still, most people need to overcome their fears and find the courage to do daily tasks. Selling takes courage.

Fear is an emotion we all struggle with; there are countless times in our lives when we let fear impact our decisions. In an earlier section, we talked about uncertainty and anxiety; these two intertwined forces are tied directly to your ability to manage fear. Fear is related to the risk associated with a future event or situation. Fear can be a healthy emotion that keeps us from physical harm, but it also commonly leads to the wrong decision.

Fear of Losing

In sales, as in life, fear can lead us to shortsighted, harmful, or desperate decisions and actions. Taking actions based on fear of losing a deal, such as discounting, means you've likely already lost. It undermines our confidence which often leads us to desperate actions. When we let this happen, it can lead us to 'winning' a bad deal, a deal where we have cut our profits and given ourselves little room to operate profitably. This can create unnecessary tension, stress, and undermine the customer relationship. It also sets up the customer to have wrong expectations going forward. Just like a loss can be a win, a win can be a loss.

The correct answer is to slow down and sell more. Don't be afraid to lose a deal; clients can sense desperation. If you believe in what you are selling and its value, if you have differentiated yourself through the sales process, you must find confidence. Sell without fear. Sell courageously.

Becoming a Lion

Courage gives confidence and leads to better outcomes; it empowers you to negotiate for an actual win-win outcome. It sets the right expectation with customers, one where they respect the value of the product and services you are selling.

Courage allows us to build trust from a position of power while remaining humble. Some people might think of courage and humility as opposites, but I would argue differently. They are two forces that work together. For example, sharing stories about a past failure or talking positively about your competitors communicates transparency, confidence, and experience, which builds trust and sets you apart from many others.

There are numerous ways we can strive to become more courageous. First, ask yourself how you'd view others dealing with the same situation. Imagine if a friend came to you with a question or issue; what sort of advice would you give to them? How would you suggest that they respond? Now apply this same advice to yourself; you already know what you need to do.

When it comes to being more courageous, it's helpful to start by identifying your strengths. Research suggests that people who focus on developing their strengths are more successful. Additionally, knowing what you're good at boosts our confidence, which in turn makes it more likely to take risks and be courageous. Simply put, when we're more confident in our abilities, we're much more willing to pursue an opportunity when it presents itself.

Another way of becoming more courageous is by understanding your goals. How are your fears getting in the way of those goals? Understanding how our fears interfere with accomplishing our goals will go far in helping you overcome them. What do you want to achieve in your professional life? What is driving you to want those things? How does fear get in the way of your goals? How would having more courage help you achieve them?

Finally, it's worth remembering that fear is a basic survival instinct designed to protect us from imminent danger. Unfortunately, fear can have the opposite of its intended effect in other circumstances, such as sales. It can get in the way of objective reality and cause us to frame things through a negative lens rather than a positive or realistic one. Ask yourself this question: "How many times have you heard fear credited for helping people become more successful?"

Standing Your Ground

Here is a somewhat common situation that most sales managers can relate to. A sales professional has been working a deal for months and they are in the final stage of hopefully closing the opportunity. There have been countless meetings, calls, emails, and lots of effort. In the eleventh hour, the customer has an objection on your consulting rate. The prospect might say something like "Your hourly consulting rate of $200 an hour is higher than your competition."

Now, this comment isn't just meant as an informational update; it is an objection requiring a response. Now, put yourself in the shoes of the sales professional who is counting on closing this big sale by year-end; they might be counting on the commission to pay for Christmas, and the obstacle is simply a discount on your rate. This happens all the time.

Now, there are times where a consulting firm undoubtedly will negotiate on rate. That said, building a relationship by having the other party say you're worth less than you think is a bad starting point.

My recommendation, respond by talking about your value, your team's experience, and NOT competing to be the cheapest choice, but instead the best. For a prospect to compare your rate to someone else, they are effectively trying to suggest that all other factors are equal. This is typically not the case.

If a prospect is looking for one of the best options and focused on value and outcomes, your rate is justified and a deal. It's important to understand that price is the ultimate decision factor only in the absence of differentiation. Harry Beckwith wrote: "If they come for the price, they'll leave for the price." If you have differentiated yourself through your approach and how you sell, don't fear price; it's relative to value. Own it! Courage and confidence are the keys.

Another typical example is when competitors get desperate and try to give away products or services for free as an introductory incentive. I view this as the 'free like a puppy' strategy. Realize that maybe you will lose, but a loss can be a win. This is a time for confidence. Respond by asking a question: "Why would they do that?"

If I have been transparent and genuinely put myself on the customer's side of the table, what is there to fear? A sales representative's fear of losing a deal is typically performance-related; it's not focused on what is best for the customer but instead on what you perceive to be best for you. Put the customer first and let the chips fall where they fall.

If you lose a deal because of standing your ground, you have lost on your terms. It is worth noting here the importance of building the foundation for this confidence. You need to have differentiated yourself through confidence, asking the right questions, listening to understand the need, and connecting with them emotionally. That empowers you to be transparent and not be ashamed about expecting to make money in a deal. Win and lose on your terms.

Bet on Yourself

The biggest business mistake I ever made was driven by fear instead of courage. When we started our company, my business partner and I left great jobs at Microsoft. The decision felt risky enough, so we opted to start the company with three local business people who were our acquaintances. We overvalued their experience and undervalued our drive, passion, and knowledge. They never invested a penny, but we all collectively signed a loan to start the business.

We wanted to part ways with them within a few years and decided to buy them out. They each made a significant amount off a zero-dollar investment. This was a painful (although valuable) lesson on courage. Don't be afraid to bet on yourself; be the master of your fate. Betting on yourself is the quickest way to success; comparatively, waiting for the world to permit you to be great is a slow path to mediocrity.

Kryptonite—Self-Doubt and the Fear of Losing

There are too many things in this world to worry about, then you have kids, and there are twice as many things in this world to worry about. Self-doubt should never be one of them; it shouldn't keep us up at night. It's impossible to know what you're capable of achieving if you don't set aside your self-doubt and try. Zig Ziglar stated, "Failure is an event, not a person."

Failure might be an event but losing sucks; it can feel like a personal rejection, cause personal financial stress, and undermine your confidence. Of course, the larger the sales opportunity, the more we feel the pressure and eyes of everyone around us. Sales professionals understand the agony of defeat as much as anyone.

There is no way of eliminating this emotion from the act of selling, and nobody bats 1,000 in sales (or baseball, for that matter). There are simple ways to improve our odds, such as asking better questions upfront to disqualify mediocre opportunities before time is wasted. More importantly, we must be okay with losing. Here is a vital lesson that took years to learn. Not every win is a win, and not every loss is a loss.

When I suggest that not every loss has to be a complete loss, I'm not suggesting some act of desperation. I am suggesting that there is a way to gain value out of these situations. When you lose a deal where you overinvested your time and were surprised by the outcome, there is a way to get something. Ask why. Understanding why you lost a deal is the proverbial opportunity to turn a lemon into lemonade.

Pick up the phone and call your contact. Preface it by saying you are constantly striving to improve, and you'd greatly appreciate 10 minutes to understand their decision better. Most deals I've ever lost were willing to give me 10 minutes. Taking advantage of a loss to learn where you went wrong allows you to improve your long-term performance. The only way to recover lost time is to learn not to make the same mistake twice. If calling yourself is awkward, have your manager or a colleague make the call on your behalf.

Additionally, it's important to remember that not every winner wins. If you showed a willingness to serve, empathy, authenticity, courage, and integrity throughout the sales process and lost, it's possible you won and just didn't know it.

I used to invest time into maintaining relationships with sales representatives that worked for our competition. Over coffee, I'd periodically hear about them winning a deal (sometimes against us) by offering significant concessions and discounts. Commonly, they would follow this up, saying we were lucky because the client was impossible to work with. You see, we were always competing to build a relationship with clients, to have a win-win outcome, not to be the cheapest option. If clients didn't value the relationship and wanted the cheapest option, letting our competition deal with those clients was absolutely a win for us! Working with a bad client can be toxic to your team and lead to employee turnover. Sometimes a loss is a win; it just takes some time and perspective to recognize it.

Final Thoughts

Courage is an equally crucial foundational skill in life. Having the courage to be vulnerable, authentic, honest, and face uncertainty head-on creates a healthy culture in any organization. Often, our fear of failure holds us back, but failure is NOT the opposite of success; failure is often a step on the path to success.

It's hard to be courageous in what you're doing if you're not sure why you're doing it. Understanding our goals gives us the clarity to recognize the difference between a brilliant opportunity and the more common distraction that gets in our way of the required focus to achieve it.

Our ability to be courageous is not a static skill; it grows stronger with practice. Like all our superpowers or any trained ability, you use it or lose it. Courageous people are the faces of who we see as great and inspirational leaders; they stand for and inspire others. They promote the truth at all costs.

Sell, lead, work, and live with courage.

Power of Dreams

"The future belongs to those who believe in the power of their dreams."

- Eleanor Roosevelt

Our final power is related to motivation; it is the power of dreams. When I say dreams, I'm not referring to the thoughts and crazy journeys we find ourselves on while we sleep. I'm referring to the other kind of dreams, the goals that drive our achievements in life. The power of dreams can be viewed as the motivation that powers your actions and gives you the drive and ambition to chase them.

We all have many dreams and aspirations as children, but eventually we start to believe we have limited power to accomplish them. We dial back our aspirations; we strive for less. Like we saw with the power of questions, we need to take some lessons from the younger version of ourselves.

There might be no greater power than that of your dreams. They function like the gas pedal in your car; they push you forward towards a goal. They provide you with the clarity of direction like a compass in our lives. They are the spark that ignites the fire within us with purpose and pushes us towards success.

Dreams allow us to reframe our future selves in a new and different light, allowing us to see past our current circumstances and view what might be possible. This lens of dreams is responsible for a lot of what has been accomplished in the world; it provides us motivation and drive.

The Triumph of High Achievement

I would suggest that no great accomplishment in history wasn't first a dream in someone's mind. Dreams are not meant to sit aimlessly on a shelf. The history books are full of men and women who faced adversity and achieved success despite it. Dreams are powerful forms of motivation but must also be paired with the necessary courage and focus to accomplish them.

I'm reminded of a favorite quote from U.S. President Theodore Roosevelt:

> *"It is not the critic who counts; not the man who points out how the strong man stumbles, or where the doer of deeds could have done them better. The credit belongs to the man who is actually in the arena, whose face is marred by dust and sweat and blood; who strives valiantly; who errs, who comes short again and again, because there is no effort without error and shortcoming; but who does actually strive to do the deeds; who knows great enthusiasms, the great devotions; who spends himself in a worthy cause; who at the best knows in the end the triumph of high achievement, and who at the worst, if he fails, at least fails while daring greatly, so that his place shall never be with those cold and timid souls who neither know victory nor defeat."*

I know a lot of entrepreneurs, and the one trait they all have in common is they dared to bet on themselves and chase a dream. You can't experience the triumph of high achievement without the courage to dare greatly.

How to Chase Your Dreams

Deciding to chase your dreams is frightening. Making changes to your life and how you live it is never easy, but achieving your dreams is possible; you just need a solid plan.

I've chased a lot of dreams. I opted for graduate school as a single parent because it was important to what I wanted to accomplish. I left a great job at a Fortune 100 company to take a chance at seeing if I could be successful as an entrepreneur. After 13 years, I sold that company to take a chance at changing my life and chasing new adventures. Each of these steps in my life started by sitting down with a pen and paper and making a list of what I wanted. You see, simply creating a list or a mission statement allows you to capture the goal.

Once you have written down your goal, you need to determine the skills and experiences you have to help you accomplish it; this allows us to assess our ability to pursue the goal. Identifying the obstacles preventing you from chasing your dreams will enable you to manage them. You probably face challenges that can directly impact your ability to be successful. Assess those challenges and decide what sacrifices you are willing to make to overcome them.

Finally, make a list of goals and the more detailed steps associated with achieving them. This will provide you with the basic framework of your plan to move forward. Start by writing down a few broad goals, then identify a few smaller steps within each one. Building a plan allows you to see the steps required to be successful, breaking it down into more manageable and achievable parts.

Dreams in Sales

Our motivations as a sales professional can be of varying size and scope. It might be related to achieving company goals or an award. It might be related to making an income that gives you the ability to buy that dream home or pay for your children's education.

A motivating job isn't the one that makes you look important or successful. It's the one that makes you feel alive and delivers upon your dreams.

Failure Isn't to Be Feared

Regret is a terrible thing; unfortunately, many people choose not to chase a dream due to fear of failure. Whether that dream is starting a new business, taking a new job, or leaving a bad one. Those people haven't learned that failure is simply a part of success. Failure is an opportunity to improve and a sign of progress if you frame it correctly. Actual failure only happens if you give up.

The more you pursue your dreams, the more the lines and boundaries that the world puts in front of us fade, as we learn that anything and everything is possible. Once we harness our dreams as motivation and take control of our fears, we are capable of almost anything.

Importance of Focus

We touched on how courage is vital in chasing our dreams. The power of focus is of equal importance. Simply put, focus is accomplished by saying no to the hundreds of distractions and other ideas that will continue to come at you.

I'm a dreamer, and in my previous company, I always threw out ideas, different directions, new product ideas, and so forth. Luckily, I had a great business partner whose role was to balance out my wild ideas. That's not to suggest they were all bad but achieving our goals meant saying no to most of them.

You must stay focused on what truly is aligned with your highest-level goals or dreams. Steve Jobs stated, "I'm actually as proud of the things we haven't done as the things we have."

Kryptonite—Fear

Unfortunately, we sometimes think that our life circumstances determine our success. This view gives us a pass from taking responsibility for our actions, inactions, and associated outcomes. Some people will suggest that the economic status you're born into affects how easy or hard it is to get ahead. I won't say this isn't true, but this view is self-sabotaging in nature; plenty of people who are born with nothing rise above their circumstances.

You might be wondering about these self-sabotaging activities I speak of. We can all relate to procrastination, negative self-talk, seeking approval, shifting the blame, undefined goals, neglecting your health, self-doubt, inaction, or just putting yourself down. There is no shortage of emotions, feelings, and thoughts that hold us back from chasing our dreams, and they are all rooted in fear. Be courageous.

Final Thoughts

Dreams are human inspiration. They motivate us to pursue what otherwise would be impossible. They ignite and stretch our imagination and give us the motivation and energy to chase great exploits. They fuel our ambitions and drive our actions.

Unlocking your dreams requires courage. Without courage, we find ourselves dismissing our dreams. We're conflicted, and so we opt for the easiest path forward. We convince ourselves and justify our actions by saying things like "It's just not meant to be," "I have responsibilities that I can't ignore," "I have to face reality."

We must work to define our dreams. We create dreams because we have a wish, and wishes come from the lack of something, a need, or an idea. Every day spent not chasing your dreams is a day lost, a day you won't get back.

Live your dreams; don't fear them.

We Should Be Good

"It's better to live with your eyes wide open and acknowledge what you can't control—while directing your attention to what you can—than it is to pretend that the things you don't wish to see don't exist."

- Zero Dean

All of us squander time on things we shouldn't be doing. Once that time is gone, it's gone forever. You can't save it or invest it. You only get time once, and that's why time is so important. It is a precious resource. Salespeople notoriously waste significant time; our optimism is like kryptonite to our superpowers. It keeps us from objectively seeing the early warning signs and chasing deals we shouldn't have.

Optimism is a double-edged sword. We need optimism in our lives; it's a considerable force that drives us forward. However, in sales, optimism can function as kryptonite, motivating us in the wrong direction and, more importantly, wasting the only resource that matters, time.

Here is a quick story. You represent one of five nationwide consulting firms competing for a large deal at a nationally known bank. One firm ruled itself out early in the process because they felt it was outside their wheelhouse. After the first round of vendor presentations, the prospective customer cut the

2nd and 3rd firms. Your firm is one of the two finalists! After numerous additional meetings and presentations, the customer selects the other firm. The thrill of victory and the agony of defeat. The question to ask is, who took second place?

Winning a competitive sales opportunity is typically an all-or-none affair. We know who took first; they won the deal, they walked away with the whole enchilada. Unfortunately, the company that lost in the final round came in last because they burned more time than any losing firm but got the same result; they got nothing. I'd rather be the firm that walked early and devoted that time towards more fruitful pursuits.

Organizations manage capital to the penny, but time is largely left unmanaged. Calendars are full of meetings that result in unintentional thievery of productivity. Steve Jobs was famous for limiting the focus of Apple to a few key priorities. Know who your prospective targets are and know who they aren't. Know the difference.

It was rare that a salesperson who worked for me ever walked into my office and said, "Just had an introductory meeting, we are not a great fit, and I am planning to cut them loose." This was the usual thing I would hear, "Just had a great first meeting! We can win this." Our optimism blinds us to the signs that, in many cases, are visible upfront. To be great at sales, you must find a way to limit the amount of time you waste. You can still be an optimist, but you can't let it blind your objectivity.

In my company, we had a saying we watched out for. The phrase was "We should be good." Listen for these words. It's a way that teams and leaders sometimes try and talk themselves into believing that something is under control or manageable; it's commonly a form of misplaced optimism. These words became a warning in my company. When someone would say "we should be good," we typically knew we weren't!

Be an optimist with equal parts objectivity.

Conclusion

I'm a salesperson. It's never been my title, but that doesn't make it less accurate. Through a lot of trial and error, I learned through selling and leading a company that sales is simply about understanding humans. It's about embracing the messy and complicated emotions instead of rigidly focusing on the logic and details. It's about not letting technology remove the human element but instead using technology to amplify and enhance it.

In putting my thoughts to paper, I came to a simple conclusion. To succeed in our roles as humans (not just salespeople or leaders), we must strive to be more connected, really connected. Our society has created more separation and individualism; social media posts have substituted for real interactions. Society has become less empathetic, and we need to reverse course. We must develop a passion for putting empathy at the center of our pursuits.

No doubt, a skilled worker can be replaced with a highly efficient AI-based machine, but automation can never be equivalent to human intelligence. It will compute faster and potentially outthink us in many ways, but machines can't replicate our ability to be empathetic, build trust, or connect with other humans. We must focus on the skills and abilities that machines can't replace, our uniquely human skills. These are the skills that will set you apart from others in sales, leadership, and countless other jobs. Remember, price is the ultimate decision-making factor in the absence of differentiation. Use your human skills to differentiate how we sell versus what we sell.

Our superpowers are the skills and abilities that only humans have. These powers might not be superhuman, but they are super powerful. We must continually engage people more profoundly by asking great questions and listening, connecting with their words, meaning, and emotion. We must put aside our egos and strive to serve others with humility and truth. We must strive to be courageous and always let our integrity rule over our ambition. We must connect with our dreams and chase the important ones.

As we become great at connecting with others, we must also become great at identifying and solving problems. This starts with understanding biases and finding ways to look at issues differently. Many of the challenges and issues that separate society today are due in part to our biases. Serving others by helping them see a situation differently is a way to change the outcome positively and fundamentally.

Finally, our journey is limited by time, and we must become masters of maximizing it. It's not about working harder but working smarter; it's about focusing our finite time to drive the most extraordinary output or result. It's about being optimistic but not making decisions based on blind optimism. We must chase our dreams with courage and focus.

As technology evolves and the world changes, the role that we each play will change. Technology will bless us with greater efficiency and productivity, but it will also feed our biases and diminish our ability to build trust. It will manipulate our beliefs and actions. Technology is a double-edged sword.

History teaches us that technology will continue to evolve and drive economic uncertainty to the working class. This does not mean there will be some battel or fisticuffs between humans and machines. It's our human abilities that give us the ultimate power over technology. Technology has a single purpose, which is to serve us. However, as jobs are replaced, we need to understand where the opportunities of tomorrow lie. We must master the skills that technology is incapable of reproducing. We should strive to let technology do what it can so we, as humans, can do what only humans can.

Strive to develop your human superpowers.

Strive to be a better human.

Sources and Further Reading

Introduction

Wikipedia contributors (2022, February 9). Industrial Revolution. In Wikipedia, The Free Encyclopedia. Retrieved 17:55, February 13, 2022, from https://en.wikipedia.org/w/index.php?title=Industrial_Revolution&oldid=1070910687.

Wikipedia contributors. "Fourth Industrial Revolution." *Wikipedia, The Free Encyclopedia*. Wikipedia, The Free Encyclopedia, December 16, 2021. Web. December 19, 2021.

Depression and Other Common Mental Disorders: Global Health Estimates. Geneva: World Health Organization; 2017. License: CC BY-NC-SA 3.0 IGO.

Ingram, T., Laforge, R., Avila, R., Schwepker, C., Williams, M. (2019) Sell[6]. Cengage

Wikipedia contributors (2022, February 10). Technological singularity. In Wikipedia, The Free Encyclopedia. Retrieved 18:11, February 13, 2022, from https://en.wikipedia.org/w/index.php?title=Technological_singularity&oldid=1071100136.

Wikipedia contributors (2022, January 21). Luddite. In Wikipedia, The Free Encyclopedia. Retrieved 18:13, February 13, 2022, from https://en.wikipedia.org/w/index.php?title=Luddite&oldid=1066982841.

How AI helps in DNA sequencing? Healthcare Tech Outlook: Thursday, July 30, 2020. How AI Helps in DNA Sequencing? (n.d.). Retrieved February 13, 2022, from https://www.healthcaretechoutlook.com /news/how-ai-helps-in-dna-sequencing-nid-1872.html.

How AI helps in DNA sequencing? Healthcare Tech Outlook: Thursday, July 30, 2020. How AI Helps in DNA Sequencing? (n.d.). Retrieved February 13, 2022, from https://www.healthcaretechoutlook.com/ news/how-ai-helps-in-dna-sequencing-nid-1872.html.

Power of Questions

Schulte, B. (2008, January 17). Ronald Reagan v. Jimmy Carter: "Are You Better Off Than You Were Four Years Ago?" US News. https://www. usnews.com/news/articles/2008/01/17/the-actor-and-the-detail-man.

Wikipedia contributors (2022, February 18). Cognitive bias. In Wikipedia, The Free Encyclopedia. Retrieved 14:56, February 19, 2022, from https://en.wikipedia.org/w/index.php?title=Cognitive_bias&oldid=10 72670312.

Power of Listening

Bodie, G. D. "The Active-Empathetic Listening Scale (AELS): Conceptualization and Evidence of Validity within the Interpersonal Domain," *Communication Quarterly* 59, no. 3 (2011): 278.

Wilding, M. Emotional Labeling: How to Control Stress and Feel Less Anxious By Naming Emotions. https://melodywilding.com/control-stress-and-feel-less-anxious-with-emotional-labeling-free-toolkit/.

Forbes, S. and Prevas, J. (2009) Power Ambition Glory: The Stunning Parallels between Great Leaders of the Ancient World and Today...and the Lessons You Can Learn. Crown Business.

Covey, S. M.R. The Speed of Trust. Free Press; New York: 2006.

Nadella, S. *Hit Refresh*. Harper Business; New York: 2017.

Power of Storytelling

Branson, R. (n.d.). Why entrepreneurs are storytellers: Virgin. Virgin.com. Retrieved February 13, 2022, from https://www.virgin.com/branson-family/richard-branson-blog/why-entrepreneurs-are-storytellers.

Wikipedia contributors (2022, February 8). Storytelling. In Wikipedia, The Free Encyclopedia. Retrieved 18:51, February 13, 2022, from https://en.wikipedia.org/w/index.php?title=Storytelling&oldid=1070704119.

Davis, M. Stories—Not Statistics—Are Memorable. https://speakingcpr.com/the-numbers-dont-lie-stories-not-statistics-make-you-memorable/#:~:text=When%20stories%20are%20used%20to%20convey%20that%20same,right%20side%20involves%20the%20emotions%20of%20the%20listener.

Stevenson, D. 2016, August 1. Why Your Brain Likes A Good Tale—The Science of Storytelling. https://www.presentation-guru.com/why-your-brain-likes-a-good-tale-the-science-of-storytelling/.

Bower, G. and Clark, M. (1969). *Narrative stories at mediators for serial learning* [online] Stanford EU. Available at: http://stanford.edu/~gbower/1969/Narrative_stories.pdf.

Power of Framing

Beckwith, H. The Invisible Touch. Warner Books; New York: 2000.

Wikipedia contributors (2021, August 24). Causal reasoning. In Wikipedia, The Free Encyclopedia. Retrieved 21:04, February 13, 2022, from https://en.wikipedia.org/w/index.php?title=Causal_reasoning&oldid=1040413870.

Wikipedia contributors. "List of cognitive biases." Wikipedia, The Free Encyclopedia. Wikipedia, The Free Encyclopedia, December 16, 2021. Web. December 19, 2021.

Cherry, K. List of Common Cognitive Biases. https://www. verywell-mind.com/cognitive-biases-distort-thinking-2794763.

Wikipedia contributors (2022, January 18). Selective perception. In Wikipedia, The Free Encyclopedia. Retrieved 21:29, February 13, 2022, from https://en.wikipedia.org/w/index.php?title=Selective_perception&oldid=1066548089.

Wikipedia contributors (2022, February 11). Halo effect. In Wikipedia, The Free Encyclopedia. Retrieved 21:32, February 13, 2022, from https://en.wikipedia.org/w/index.php?title=Halo_effect&oldid=1071178656.

Wikipedia contributors (2021, November 18). Framing effect (psychology). In Wikipedia, The Free Encyclopedia. Retrieved 21:33, February 13, 2022, from https://en.wikipedia.org/w/index.php?title=Framing_effect_(psychology)&oldid=1055848123.

Wikipedia contributors (2022, February 10). Sunk cost. In Wikipedia, The Free Encyclopedia. Retrieved 21:35, February 13, 2022, from https://en.wikipedia.org/w/index.php?title=Sunk_cost&oldid=1071089727.

Power of Serving

Salz, L. *Sales Differentiation*. HarperCollins Leadership; New York: 2018.

Wikipedia contributors (2021, November 26). Caveat emptor. In Wikipedia, The Free Encyclopedia. Retrieved 20:17, January 23, 2022, from https://en.wikipedia.org/w/index.php?title=Caveat_emptor&oldid=1057198742.

Wikipedia contributors (2022, February 12). Altruism. In Wikipedia, The Free Encyclopedia. Retrieved 21:50, February 13, 2022, from https://en.wikipedia.org/w/index.php?title=Altruism&oldid=1071423411.

Power of Focus

Gilbert DT. *Stumbling on Happiness*. Random House; New York: 2006.

McAleese, S. The Power of Focus. https://medium.com/swlh/the-power-of-focus-b6d91f5735cd.

Power of Empathy

Mayer, D., Greenberg, H. What Makes a Good Salesman. https://hbr.org/2006/07/what-makes-a-good-salesman.

Wikipedia contributors (2022, February 14). Empathy. In Wikipedia, The Free Encyclopedia. Retrieved 01:38, February 15, 2022, from https://en.wikipedia.org/w/index.php?title=Empathy&oldid=1071833634.

Street RL Jr., Makoul G, Arora NK, Epstein RM. How does communication heal? Pathways linking clinician–patient communication to health outcomes. Patient Educ Couns. 2009;74:295–301.

Power of Truth

Aristotle. *Rhetoric* (W. Rhys Roberts, Translator). (Mineola, New York: Dover Publications, Inc., 2004). 1355a20.

Robbins, M. The Power of Authenticity. https://www.oprah.com/spirit/the-power-of-authenticity/all.

Power of Courage

Gordon, S. 7 Ways to Feel More Courageous. https://www.verywellmind.com/7-ways-to-feel-more-courageous-5089058.

Muthoni, J. Why Courage is Important. https://jonasmuthoni.com/blog/importance-of-courage/.

Power of Dreams

Blake, K. 5 Things I've Learned About Chasing Your Dreams. https://www.huffpost.com/entry/5-things-learned-about-chasing-your-dreams_b_5578108.

Alford, C. 11 Reasons Why It's Important to Follow Your Dreams. https://www.lifehack.org/articles/communication/11-reasons-why-its-important-follow-your-dreams.html.